# HOT SITES

## paper-surf

## the superhighway

general editor · roger walton

# HOT SITES

First published in 1997 by:
Hearst Books International
1350 Avenue of the Americas
New York, NY 10019
United States of America

Distributed in the United States
and Canada by:
Watson-Guptill Publications
1515 Broadway
New York, NY 10036

US ISBN 0-688-15888-9

First published in Germany by:
NIPPAN
Nippon Shuppan Hanbai
Deutschland GmbH
Krefelder Str. 85
D–40549 Düsseldorf
Telephone: (0211) 5048089
Fax: (0211) 5049326

German ISBN 3-931884-11-2

First published in Singapore by:
Page One Publishing Pte Ltd
Blk 4 #08-37 Pasir Panjang Road
Alexandra Distripark, Singapore 118491
Telephone: 65-2743188
Fax: 65-2741833

Singaporean ISBN 981-00-9222-9

Distributed throughout the rest of the world by:
Hearst Books International
1350 Avenue of the Americas
New York, NY 10019

ISBN 0-688-15774-2

Edited and designed by
Duncan Baird Publishers
75–76 Wells Street, London W1P 3RE
e-mail: roger@dbairdpub.co.uk

Managing Designer: Gabriella Le Grazie
Designer: Jeniffer Harte
Assistant Designer: Richard Horsford
Editor: Clare Richards
Researcher: Max Bielenberg

10 9 8 7 6 5 4 3 2 1

Typeset in Helvetica Condensed
Color reproduction by Colourscan, Singapore
Printed in Hong Kong

< > When these arrows appear next to page numbers
they indicate that the artwork has been displayed
horizontally rather than vertically.

# foreword

> at last the net is cool. new media technology is no longer the exclusive domain of pioneering programmers and technical experts – ground-breaking design is now being woven into the texture of the digital realm.

> estimates of the number of internet addresses by the year 2000 range from 100 to 200 million, indicating two things: the internet is an incredibly powerful medium, and no one yet knows quite how spectacular its growth will be. already, millions of dollars are being invested each year in a design activity that did not exist a decade ago, as new web sites appear daily and cd roms evolve as a cost-effective means of communication.

> the learning curve in web-site and cd-rom design has been steep. from the relatively recent days of its basic and mundane appearance, design for the new media has forged ahead to create its own aesthetic, which now, in turn, influences not only tv graphics but also design for printed media.

> the collection presented here gathers together web sites and cd roms that have been created to fulfill a range of objectives: promotion for products and retail brands in the digital equivalent of magazine advertorials; online advertising for services and events; and information across the broadest imaginable spectrum. also included, and shown for the first time, are experimental pieces from small companies and individuals which demonstrate that innovation is often the result of imagination and flair rather than large budgets.

> **HOT SITES** freeze-frames today's most inspiring and provocative screen work, providing an invaluable record of an extraordinarily creative period in design history.

< 7

r.w.

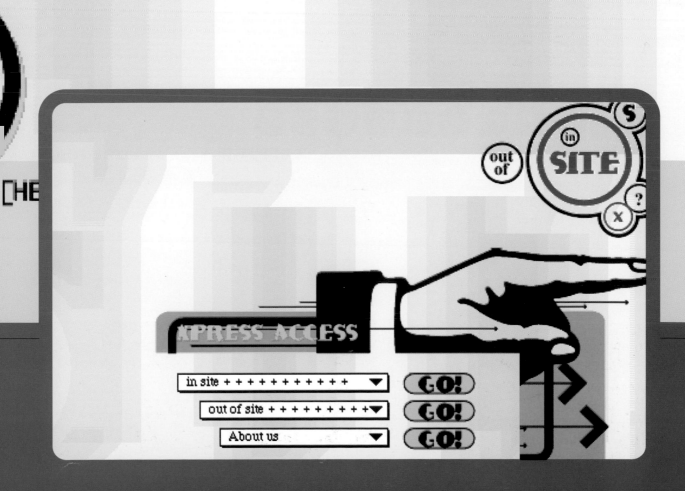

**title**
the site

**address**
www.thesite.org.uk

**client**
youthnet

**number of pages**
1000+

**design**
neil clavin

**design company**
webmedia

**programming**
webdevelopment

**software**
debabelizer, illustrator, mediasurface,
photoshop

**origin**
uk

**work description**
online advice centre providing
guidance to young people on
social and personal issues

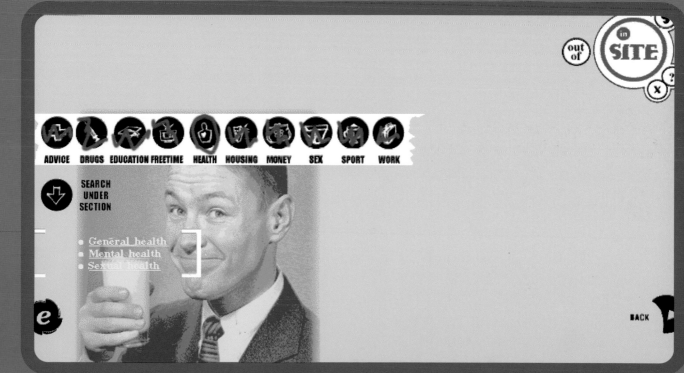

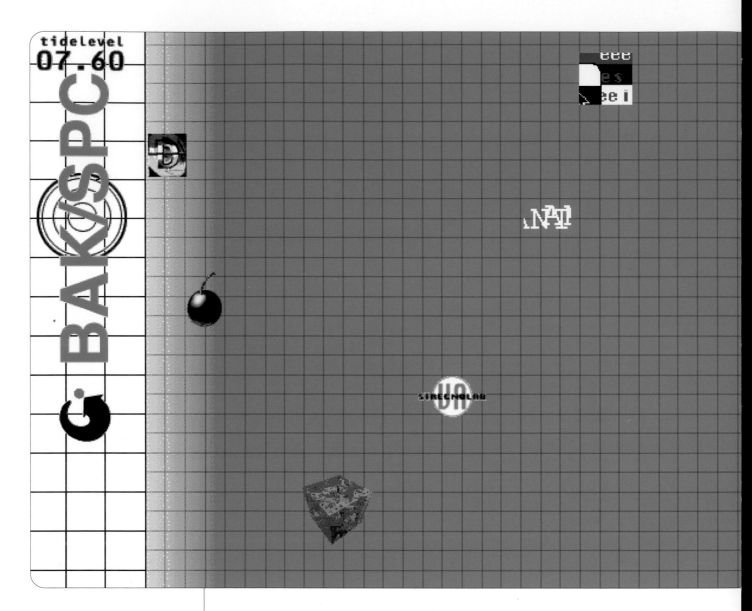

tidelevel
07.60

BAK/SPC

14

STRECNOLAB

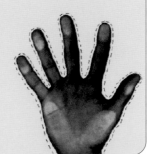

in·active artworks

return

instructions

1. cut around the dotted line, (perhaps use a sharp knife).

2. stick to the palm of your hand, (be sure to use a sutable strong adesive).

3. interact (wave at somebody).

ビックサンの
旅行　BIGSONS TRAVELS

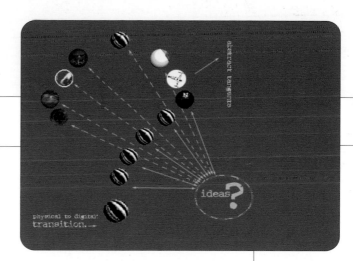

**title**
bigson's travels

**address**
www.backspace.org/bigson/

**design**
bigson (james gibson)

**design company**
j-buyers

**illustration**
bigson

**photography**
bigson

**programming**
bigson

**software**
bbedit, photoshop,
sound edit

**origin**
uk

**work description**
online collection of journal
extracts, thoughts,
observations, and artwork

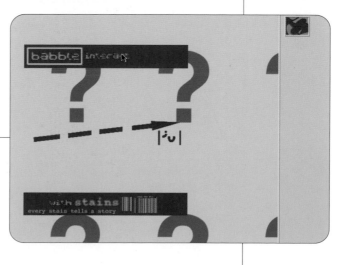

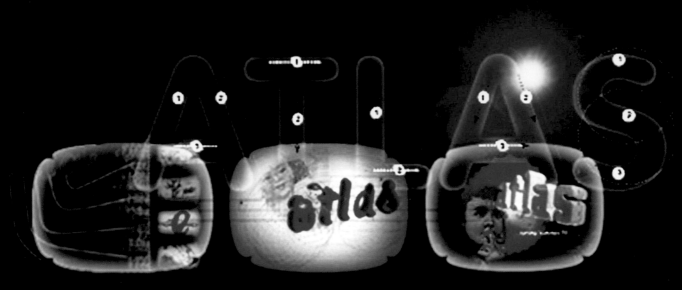

# ATLAS

cyberBILLY photography editorial paradise online
*winter 97*

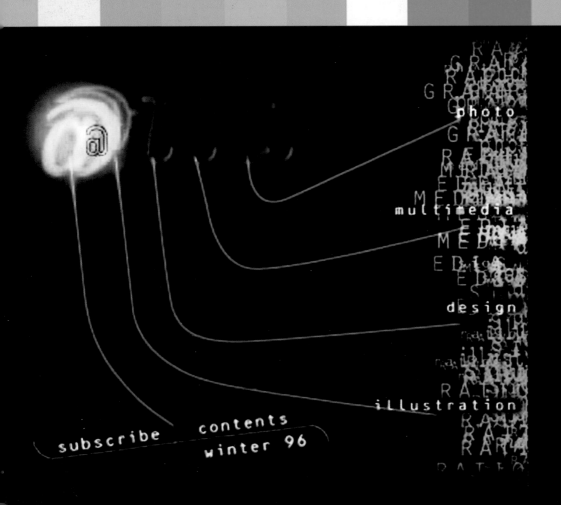

@

photo
multimedia
design
illustration

subscribe contents
*winter 96*

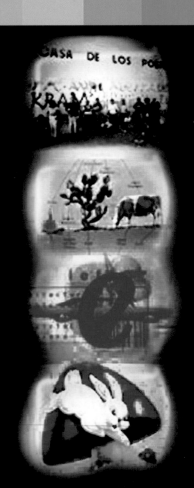

CASA DE LOS PO

PHOTO | MULTIMEDIA | DESIGN | ILLUSTRATION

pages 18–19

**title**
post/tv

**address**
www.posttool.com

**number of pages**
30

**design**
david karam, gigi biederman,
tom bland, stella lai

**design company**
post tool design

**illustration**
david karam, gigi biederman, stella lai

**photography**
todd hido

**programming**
david karam

**software**
after effects, bbedit, debabelizer, director,
gifbuilder, illustrator, infini-d, netscape
with shockwave, photoshop

**origin**
usa

**work description**
promotional info-tainment site

17

**title**
@tlas magazine

**address**
www.atlasmagazine.com

**design**
ame francescini

**design companies**
post tool design, @tlas design,
future farmers of america

**programming**
michael macrone

**software**
after effects, bbedit, debabelizer, director,
gifbuilder, illustrator, infini-d, netscape
with shockwave, photoshop

**origin**
usa

**work description**
portfolio-based site for designers,
illustrators, and photo-journalists

post /tv

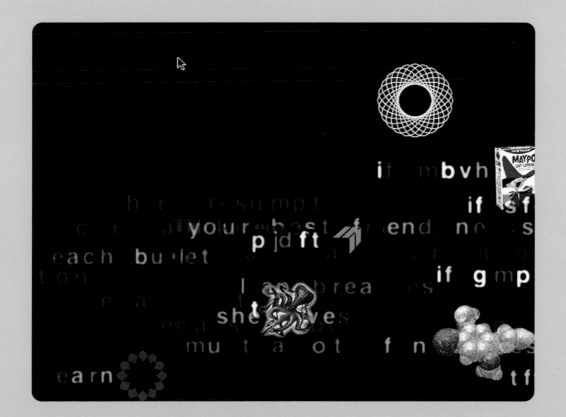

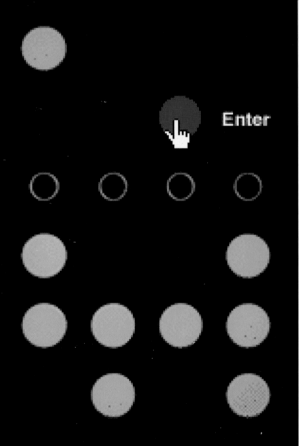

Enter

# Form

3 Long Yard, London. WC1N 3LU
Telephone: 0171 404 8621  Fax: 0171 404 1201

ISDN: 0171 405 4849  e-mail: Form@dircon.co.uk
http://www.form.uk.com

**Design/Art Direction**

**title**
form web site

**address**
www.form.uk.com

**number of pages**
81

**art direction**
paul west, paula benson

**design**
lisa smith

**design company**
form

**software**
freehand, gifbuilder, infini-d
pagemill, photoshop

**origin**
uk

**work description**
promotional portfolio web site for a
design company

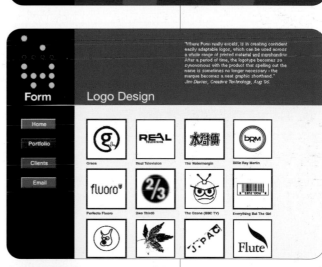

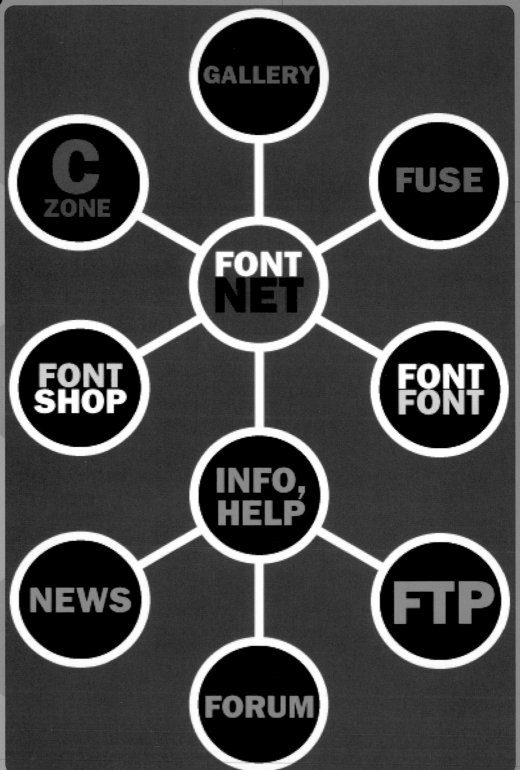

FONT
NET
http://www.type.co.uk/

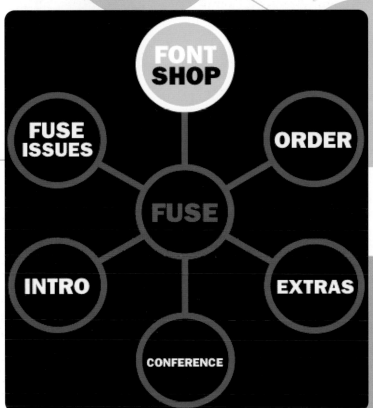

title
fontnet

address
www.type.co.uk

client
fontworks uk ltd

number of pages
400+

art direction
neville brody

design
neville brody, mike williams

design company
research arts

programming
dave barr

software
acrobat, bbedit, director, freehand,
netscape commerce server, photoshop

origin
uk

work description
online profile of a digital typefoundry's
products and services

23

FONTNET **F•1-15**

# FUSE
The interactive magazine

| 1 | 2 | 3 | 4 |
| 5 | 6 | 7 | 8 |
| 9 | 10 | 11 | 12 |
| 13 | 14 | 15 | CD |

| EXITS | FRAMES OFF | SITE OVERVIEW | SEARCH | NEWS | LOCAL TIME |

**Font Shop**

# Wir bringen
# Schrift zur Sprache

Neu: <u>Downloads</u>

| HOME | SHOPS | SERVICE | HOTLINE | KONFERENZ |
|---|---|---|---|---|
| FontShop | FontBook | BookShop | ShopShop | TYPO 96 FUSE 95 |

24

**Nur bei FontShop:**
**FontBook und FontBook Band 2**
Die größte Schriftübersicht
seit Erfindung des Buchdrucks.

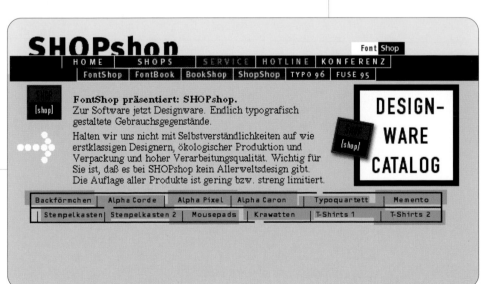

**title**
fontshop deutschland

**address**
www.fontshop.de

**client**
fontshop germany

**number of pages**
60

**design**
tina frank

**design company**
u.r.l.

**programming**
peter meininger

**software**
bbedit, debabelizer,
photoshop

**origin**
germany

**work description**
promotional web site for a
font mail order company

25

**title**
inwirements

**address**
www.frank.co.at/frank

**client**
inwirements, mego, m.dos

**number of pages**
15

**design**
tina frank

**design company**
inwirements

**programming**
andreas pieper, tina frank

**software**
bbedit, debabelizer,
makromedia, photoshop

**origin**
austria

**work description**
promotional web site for a
design company

26

27

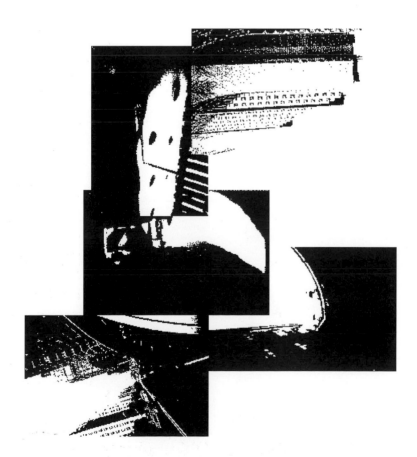

the show

leave your stories here

leave your sounds here

This event was broadcast live by Virgin Net

## www.vwo.mcg.gla.ac.uk  virtu

go to the vwo diary of stories

... this site has been accessed by people from more than **160** countries ...

nva organisation

**title**
virtual world orchestra

**address**
www.vwo.mcg.gla.ac.uk

**number of pages**
55

**art direction**
angus farquhar

**design**
stefan korn

**illustration**
locofoco

**programming**
stefan korn

**software**
photoshop

**origin**
uk

**work description**
educational and information web site
featuring stories sent in from more than
160 countries

world orchestra

world orchestra

virtual world orchestra ● diary of stories

**stories from the fruitmarket - friday 4/4/97**

**inside** - trip to paris
**outside** - nothing boring life
**future** - not to different. technology will be different especially in medicine. higher intellect and more open sexual relations.
**name** - julia

**inside** - moving away from home when i went to university. i was able to do what i wanted.
**outside** - the manchester bombing almost killed my family.
**future** - environment wont be working. everything will be damaged. people will be become more selfish.
**name** - emily

**inside** - my girlfriends brother announced his girlfriend was pregnant.
**outside** - the general election. i dont want a labour government. it will have a large impact.
**future** - communicatio will be the key to our future lives and will dictate our lives. language will not be a problem.
**name** - david irvine

**inside** - in town doing boring things in town and went to a friends house to show an essay20 minutes later and i was suprised as sombody i had not seen for a long time was there.
**outside** - not much happening locally.
**future** - its going to be very good or very bad. we destroy or liberate ourselves.
**name** - leo southwell

**inside** - loss and grief.
**outside** - going to st andrews and sat on the beach.
**future** - it is ungraspable. you cannot predict it.

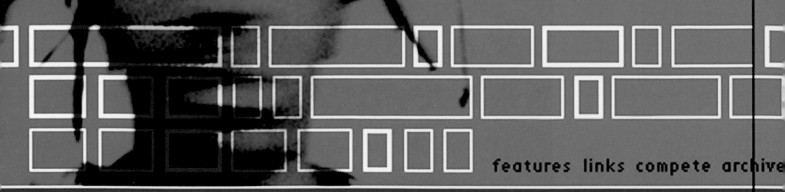

features links compete archive

production + contributor information + other 1AB projects coming to you soon

# *raise* #2|02:97|print #2.1|18:02:97|digital

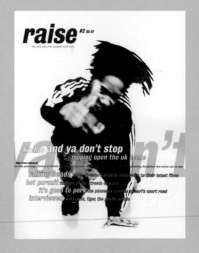

**title**
raise magazine web site

**address**
www.raise.co.uk

**client**
onearmbandit

**number of pages**
100+

**art direction**
mark hough, philip o'dwyer

**design**
philip o'dwyer

**design company**
1ab

**programming**
philip o'dwyer, phil webster

**software**
bbedit, director, pagemill, photoshop

**origin**
uk

**work description**
web site accompanying a lifestyle magazine. the navigation interface is based on a pagemap of the printed magazine that transforms into a site map, signposting the areas of the magazine that are expanded online

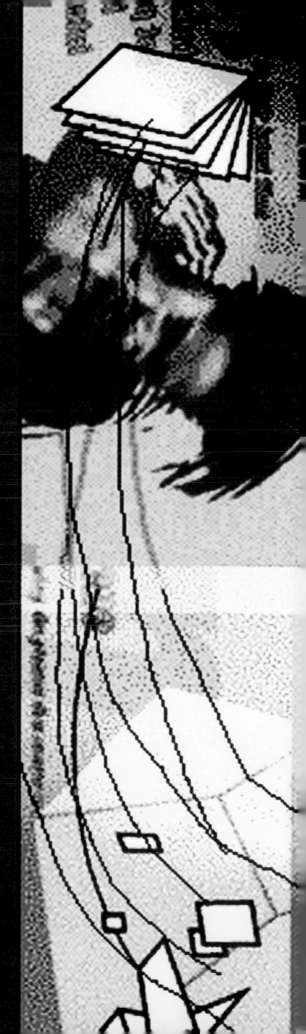

# raise

#2 | 02:97 | print   #2.1 | 18:02:97 | digital

hip-hop: \ and ya don't stop

**title**
typewriter

**address**
www.alpertawards.com/typewriter

**design**
michael worthington

**programming**
michael worthington

**software**
director, fontographer, sound edit

**origin**
usa

**work description**
unpublished web site displaying
the beat gothic typeface in its
three weights

kleber design things

recycle
+ aesth

julian

kylie n

stereo

warp r

source

gener

china

oscilla

metal

hydrog

**title**
kleber

**address**
www.kleber.co.uk/

**design**
chris mcgrail, dorian moore

**design company**
kleber

**programming**
chris mcgrail, dorian moore

**software**
bbedit, freehand, photoshop

**origin**
uk

**work description**
promotional web site for a
design company

# büro destruct

[gymnastics]
[gimmicks]
[publications]
[bd rom]
[bd fonts]
[DDD]
[classic coffee page]
[guestbook]
[links]
[mail]

*above and pages 38–9*

**title**
büro destruct homepage

**address**
www.bermuda.ch/bureaudestruct

**number of pages**
95

**design**
lopetz, heiwid

**design company**
büro destruct

**programming**
daniel schüler, rémy blandeau, heiwid

**software**
irix, linux, netscape navigator, s.u.s.e., vi

**origin**
switzerland

**work description**
promotional web site for a design company

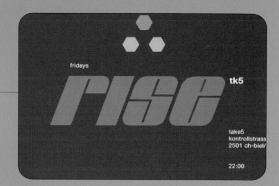

fridays

**rise** tk5

take5
kontrollstrass
2501 ch-biel/

22:00

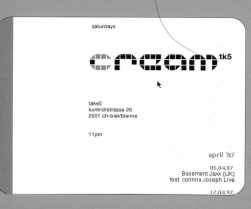

saturdays

**cream** tk5

take5
kontrollstrasse 26
2501 ch-biel/bienne

11pm

april '97

05.04.97
Basement Jaxx (UK)
feat. corinna Joseph Live

12.04.97

**title**
perron 8/take 5

**address**
www.bermuda.ch/tk5/

**client**
perron 8

**number of pages**
10

**design**
lopetz

**design company**
büro destruct

**programming**
daniel schüler

**software**
irix, linux, netscape navigator,
s.u.s.e., vi

**origin**
switzerland

**work description**
promotional web site for
an organizer of club-nights,
open-air cinema, and fashion
events

# tk5

take5
kontrollstrasse 26
2501 ch-biel/bienne

take**5**

**rise cream** ■

fridays     saturdays

bookings
artist informations

flyer gallery

elk font basics
@lopetz im büro destruct

[[.:::                                    :::.]]

<&l.::: elk:siTe:::.,>

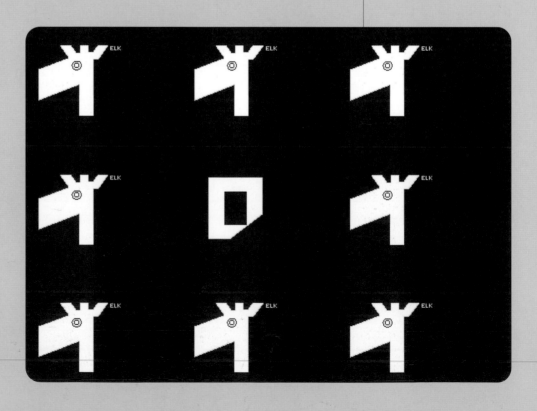

GYMNΑSTICS

STORMY WATERS

**title**

east west

**address**

www.stormy-waters.co.uk

**client**

nva

**design**

mark breslin

**software**

freehand

**origin**

uk

**work description**

artwork providing a visual backdrop to
a multimedia performance event

*pages 42–3*

**title**
yo yo men

**address**
www.stormy-waters.co.uk

**client**
nva

**design**
mark breslin

**software**
freehand

**origin**
uk

**work description**
artwork providing a visual
backdrop to a multimedia
performance event

41

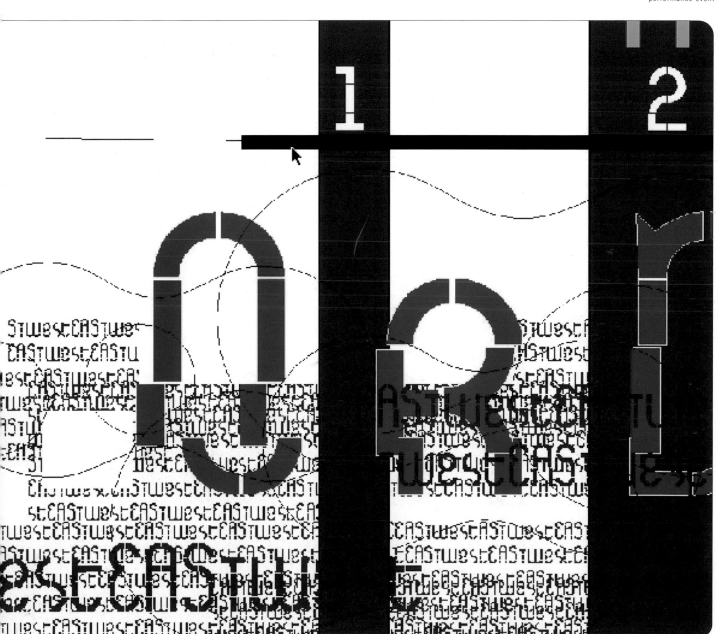

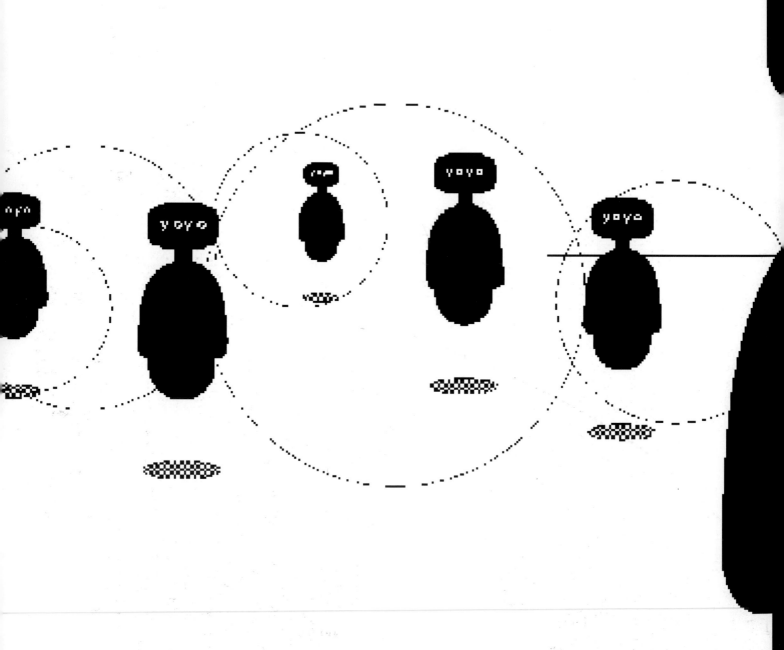

You cannot not communicate:
welcome to the MetaCulture

info@metadesign.com

MetaDesign

MetaWho? Projects Clients Type MetaCulture

< 44

**work description**

promotional web site for a multi-disciplinary design company. the site acts as both a marketing vehicle and a recruitment tool, presenting information about the firm, its clients projects, and philosophy

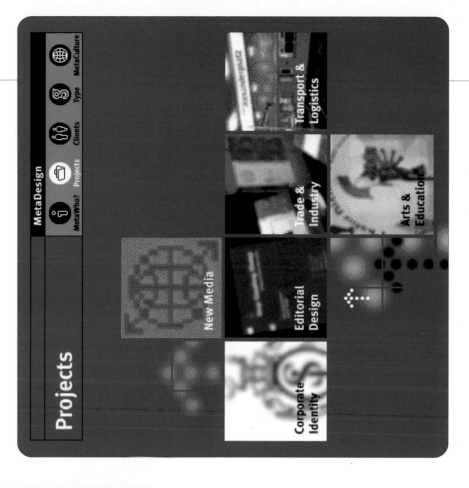

Projects

MetaWho? | Projects | Clients | Type | MetaCulture

MetaDesign

Transport & Logistics

Trade & Industry

Arts & Education

New Media

Editorial Design

Corporate Identity

# MetaDesign

## is a method, not just a style

MetaDesign is a multidisciplinary design firm with offices in San Francisco, Berlin, and London.

Our vision is an international network of visual engineers, bringing a broad cultural perspective to the complex problems of everyday communication.

**title**
metadesign web site

**address**
www.metadesign.com

**number of pages**
200+

**art direction**
rick lowe, terry irwin

**design**
conor mangat

**photography**
jym warhol, kevin ng, anne valva

**design company**
metadesign

**programming**
annie valva, conor manga, kevin farnham, joseph teries

**software**
bbedit, director, illustrator, photoshop, shockwave

**origin**
usa

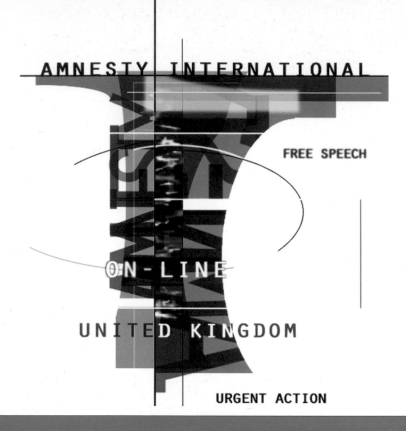

**title**
amnesty uk

**address**
www.amnesty.co.uk

**client**
amnesty uk

**design**
william julien

**design company**
sunbather

**software**
debabelizer, illustrator, photoshop

**origin**
uk

**work description**
information web site

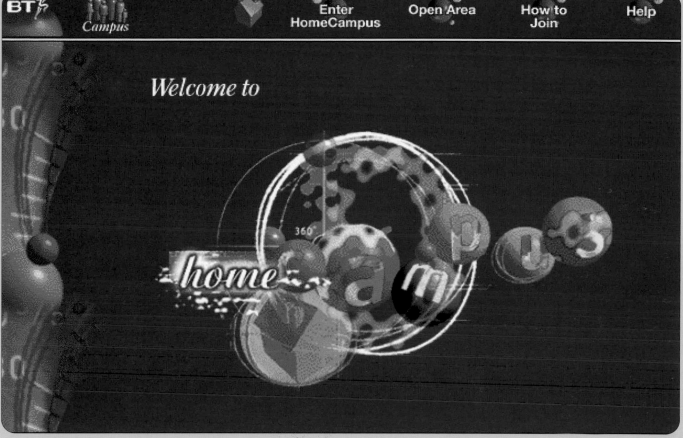

**title**
bt homecampus

**address**
www.campus.bt.com:81/homecampus/

**client**
bt

**number of pages**
50+

**art direction**
paul sonley

**design**
paul sonley, anj medhurst

**design company**
sunbather

**illustration**
paul sonley, stuart maccallum

**software**
debabelizer, extreme 3d, illustrator,
photoshop

**origin**
uk

**work description**
educational web site incorporating
colorful graphics, shockwave movies,
and java animations

title
swatch web site

address
www.swatch.com

art direction
roberto costa

design
roberto costa

design company
albert bloser, roberto costa

swatch communication lab, new york

programming
id-gruppe (germany)

origin
usa

work description
promotional web site

**title**
the official pages of audi

**address**
www.audi.de

**client**
audi ag, ingolstadt

**number of pages**
600+

**art direction**
charly frech

**design**
richard buhl, eva nagl

**design company**
metadesign plus gmbh (germany)

**programming**
hassan es said

**software**
bbedit, debabelizer, photoshop

**origin**
germany

**work description**
promotional web site

| site map |

event
technology
environment
design
safety
tradition

Audi Careers
Audi Clubs
International Auto Shows
Audi Safe-Driver Training Programm
Audi Importers Worldwide
Audi Mail

Audi database

report  models  service  facts  news

Audi A8
Audi A6
Audi A4
Audi A3
Audi Cabriolet

Locations
Annual Report
Audi History

Audi

site map
site map
site map

navigation
copyright

tim henman

*opposite, top*

**title**
homepage issue 10

**address**
www.adidas.com

**number of pages**
4500+

**design**
dusty mcsheffrey, jaki porter

**photography**
allsports

**programming**
james waite

**software**
simple text

**origin**
uk

**work description**
sports web site

*opposite, bottom*

**title**
1997 running

**address**
www.adidas.com

**number of pages**
4500+

**design**
les welch

**illustration**
kathy stimpson

**photography**
adidas

**programming**
kathy stimpson

**software**
homepage

**origin**
uk

**work description**
sports web site

*above*

**title**
homepage issuc 12

**address**
www.adidas.com

**number of pages**
4500+

**design**
jaki porter

**illustration**
jaki porter

**programming**
nina balogh

**software**
bbedit

**origin**
uk

**work description**
sports web site

welcome
to the
Hi5
FIVE

web site

Summary

Arjo Wiggins

**title**
hi-five web site for arjo wiggins fine papers

**address**
www.hi5.co.uk

**client**
arjo wiggins fine papers

**number of pages**
40

**art direction**
luc besner

**design**
nicolas izarn

**design company**
reflex design

**photography**
ranon escoba

**origin**
france

the Hi-five gallery

**work description**

promotional web site for a range of colored papers and boards, where designers can exhibit and view work

tekconnect

welcome

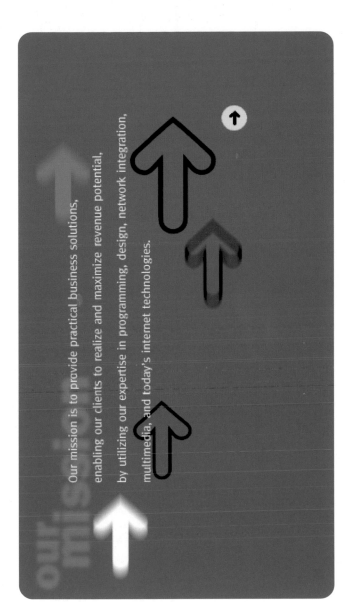

Our mission is to provide practical business solutions, enabling our clients to realize and maximize revenue potential, by utilizing our expertise in programming, design, network integration, multimedia, and today's internet technologies.

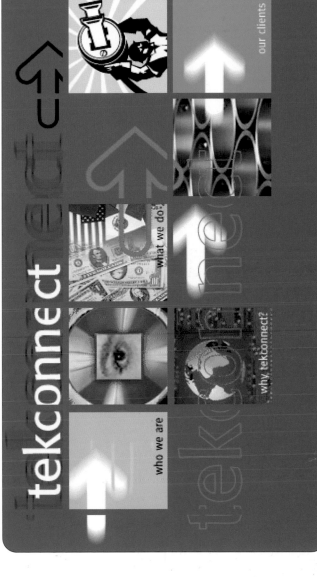

our clients

what we do?

why tekconnect?

who we are

tekconnect

**title**
tekconnect internetworks web site

**address**
www.tekconnect.net

**client**
tekconnect internetworks

**number of pages**
25

**design**
david decheser

**design company**
dreamless studios, tekconnect

**illustration**
joseph hasenauer

**programming**
david decheser

**software**
debabelizer, frontpage, illustrator, photoshop

**origin**
usa

**work description**
promotional web site for an internet solutions provider, with information on internet issues

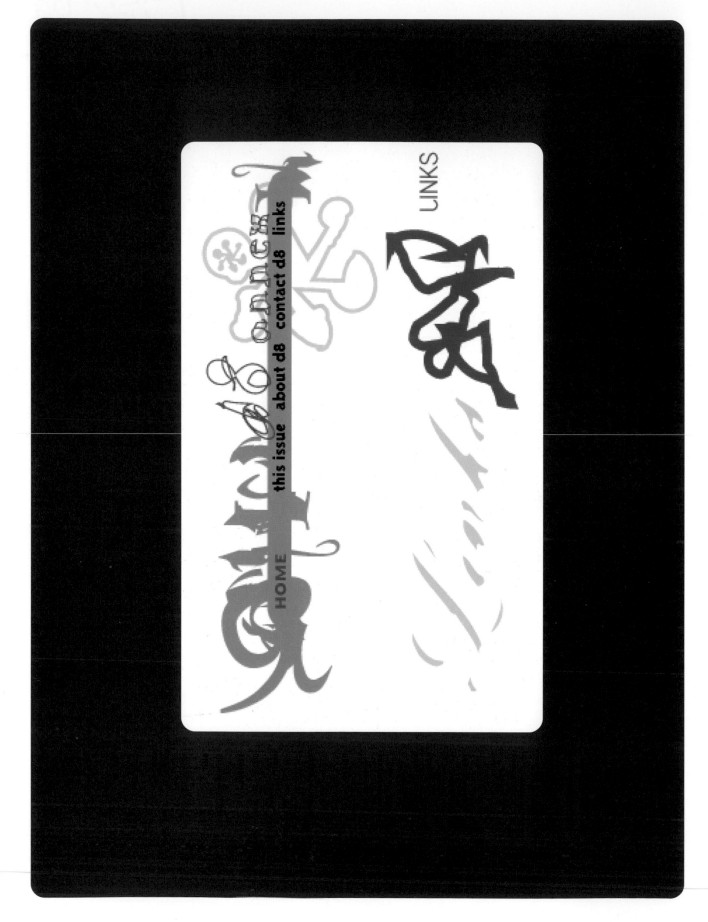

LINKS

HOME   this issue   about d8   contact d8   links

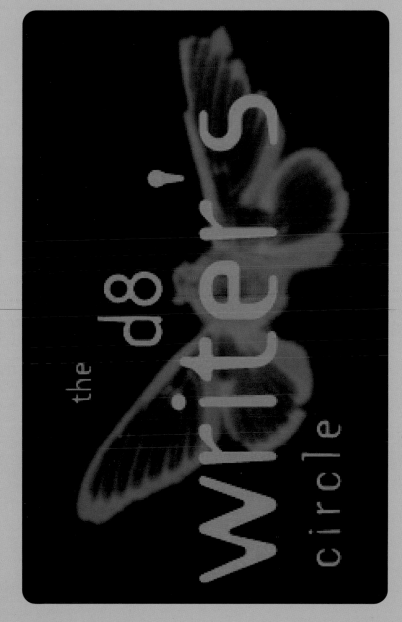

the d8 writers' circle

**work description**
promotional web site for
the printed version
of a role-playing
magazine

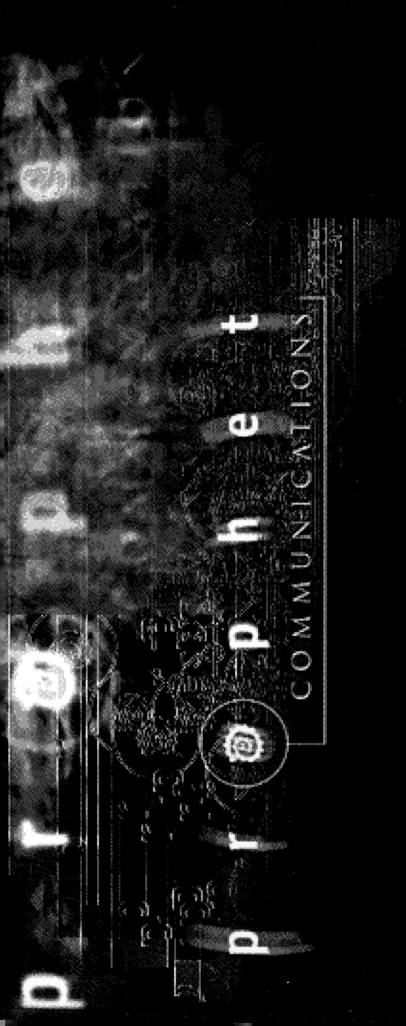

prophet

COMMUNICATIONS

In the Electronic Age
we wear all humankind as our skin.

There is a new opportunity
our true natures by the media we create,
We reveal
absorb,
need.

to extend our physical senses outward,
to explore virgin territory.

Prophet will lead the way.

ICONOCLASM

WHERE HAVE ALL THE
DESIGNERS GONE?

WE HAVE COME TO EXPECT
ASTOUNDING THINGS. IT IS REMARKABLE
HOW THE TIMES HAVE BEEN SUBVERSIVE PRINT DESIGN
AND SOMETIMES EVEN SUBVERSIVE PRINT DESIGN

DAVID CARSON, EMIGRE, P. SCOTT MAKELA.

**title**
prophet communications web site

**address**
www.prophetcomm.com

**number of pages**
21

**art direction**
josh feldman

**design**
josh feldman, thor muller

**design company**
prophet communications

**programming**
jason monburg

**software**
bbedit, illustrator,
infini-d, photoshop

**origin**
usa

**work description**
promotional web site for a design company

· **EXPLORE WITHIN** ·

**title**
bau-da design lab, inc. online portfolio

**address**
www.bauda.com

**number of pages**
40+

**design**
p.r. brown

**design company**
bau-da design lab, inc.

**illustration**
p.r. brown

**programming**
eric brown @ readynetgo, inc.

**software**
director, illustrator, photoshop

**origin**
usa

**work description**
promotional web site for a design
company which can be personalized
for the individual user

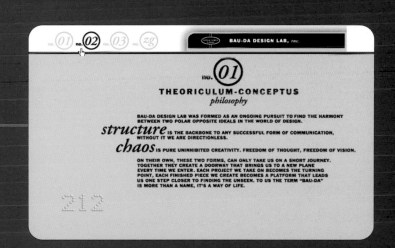

VERSIONS | 日本語 | I | O 360° | デジタル デザイン
DIGITAL DESIGN INCORPORATED
NEW YORK CITY USA

Our experiments. Requires Netscape 2.0+, java, VRML 1.0 and the following plug-ins: mBED, shockwave 5.0, Real Audio 3.0 and Futurewave.

Our clients. Netscape 1.1 or equivalent browser. Nothing painful, we promise. Easy Bandwidth.

EMPLOYMENT OPPORTUNITIES

YO

OY

?

WHAT'S NEW

Copyright 1996 i/o 360
Made with mksite 2.1

*pages 62–5*

**title**
i/o 360 digital design, inc.

**address**
www.io360.com

**number of pages**
100+

**design**
gong szeto, nam szeto,
dindo magallanes, arek bonasik

**design company**
i/o 360

**programming**
steve kann

**software**
emacs, gifbuilder,
mksite, photoshop, vi

**origin**
usa

**work description**
portfolio web site for a design company

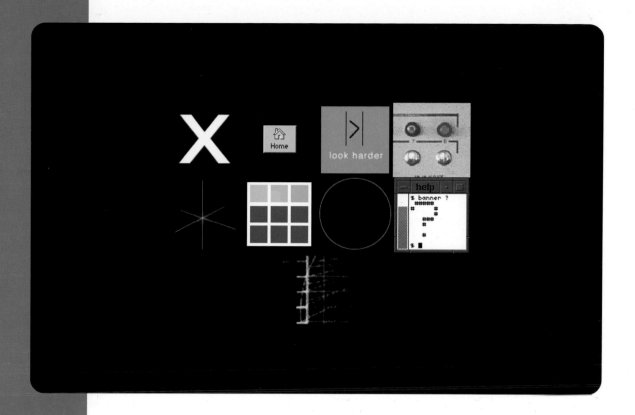

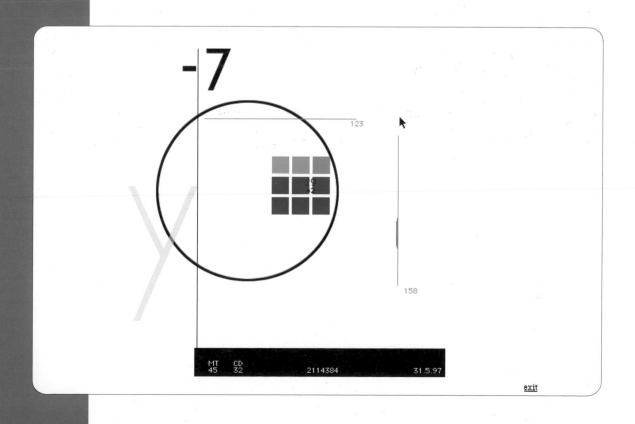

360 digital design
new york.

# /projects

An Installation:
Variations on Cryptography

Web:
The E-Ville Dialogues | Āporia

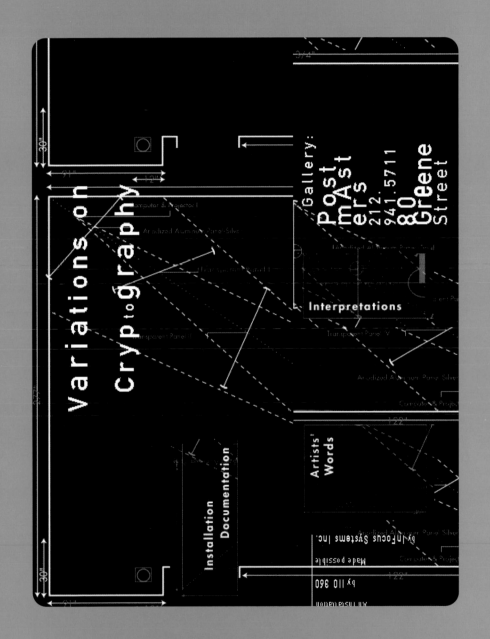

Variations on Cryptography

Gallery:
Post
mAst
ers
212.
941.5711
80
Greene
Street

Interpretations

Artists' Words

Installation Documentation

| Space | Work | Information | E-Mail | **Home** |

**Radio Internationale Stadt**
Audio on demand in real time
via internet.

**title**
moniteurs web site

**address**
www.icf.de/moniteurs

**number of pages**
30

**design**
heike nehl, sibylle schlaich,
heidi specker

**design company**
moniteurs

**programming**
moniteurs, andreas pieper

**software**
csound, director/shockwave, photoshop,
ptoa, real audio, simple text

**origin**
germany

**work description**
promotional web site for a design company

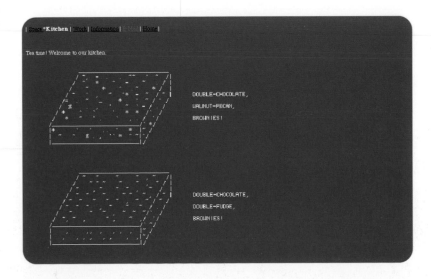

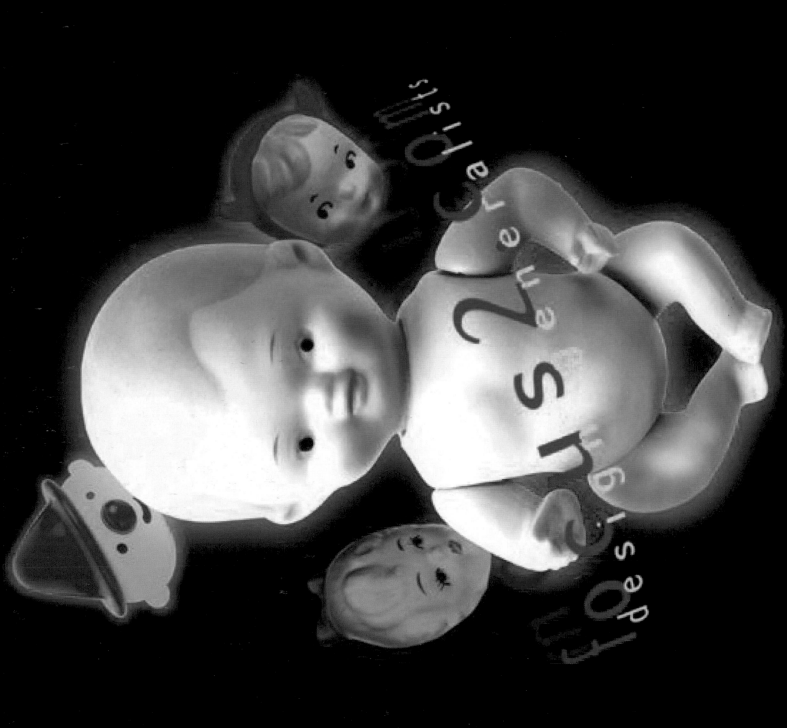

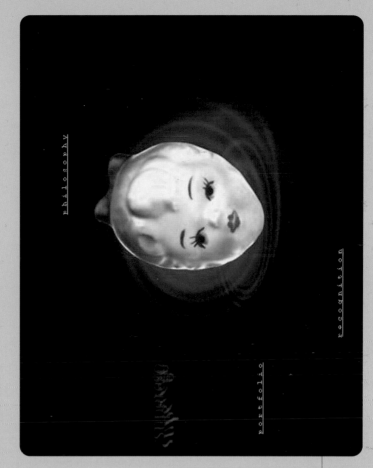

philosophy

portfolio

recognition

**work description**
promotional web site communicating
the philosophy and services of a
cross-media architectural firm

**title**
focus2 – crossmedia architects

**address**
www.focus2.com

**number of pages**
50+

**design**

shawn freeman, todd hart,
cort langworthy, brad walton

**design company**
focus2

**illustration**
shawn freeman, cort langworthy

**photography**
dick patrick, jake dean, richard seagraves

**programming**
david adams, walker hale iv

**software**
bbedit, codewarrior, illustrator, pagemill,
photoshop

**origin**
usa

**title**
speak magazine web site

**address**
www.speakmag.com/speakmag/

**art direction**
martin venezky

**design**
david granvold

**origin**
usa

**work description**
promotional web site accompanying
a printed magazine

/speakup.com

5 3 > Cool-Ass

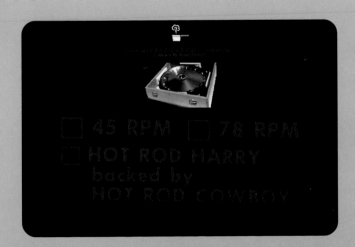

☐ 45 RPM  ☐ 78 RPM
☐ HOT ROD HARRY
backed by
HOT ROD COWBOY

all images

**title**
house of blues web site

**design**
dave bravenec

**design company**
hob new media

**illustration**
dave bravenec

**photography**
dave bravenec

**programming**
ian nguyen

**software**
illustrator, photoshop

**origin**
usa

all images except right

**work description**
event pages advertising online chats
with performing artists

72

*left*

**title**
emmylou harris

**address**
www.hob.com/events/emmylou

**client**
emmylou harris

**number of pages**
4

*right*

**title**
the fabulous thunderbirds

**address**
www.hob.com/events/birds

**client**
the fabulous thunderbirds

**number of pages**
4

**Sunset Strip House of Blues**
**July 12, 1996**
**5:00 P.M. (PDT)**

**KCSB**

**KC And The Sunshine Band**

*left*

**title**
kc and the sunshine band

**client**
kc and the sunshine band

**number of pages**
4

*far left*

**title**
speech on atlanta

**address**
www.hob.com/events/speech

**client**
house of blues

**number of pages**
3

**work description**
event site based on the java joint
web site and an interview with speech
(a musician) on the atlanta music scene

*right*

**title**
nil lara

**client**
nil lara

**number of pages**
4

73

JUNE 27, 1996
5 P.M. (PDT)

live chat

Nil

LARA

*left*

**title**
jars of clay

**address**
www.hob.com/events/jars

**client**
jars of clay

**number of pages**
4

live chat

Jars of clay

July 8, 1996
4:30 P.M. (PDT)
house of strip blues

TICKETS TO MATURITY

**title**
tickets to maturity

**number of pages**
7

**art direction**
john kariolis

**design**
john kariolis, nitesh mody

**design company**
marshall associates

**software**
photoshop

**origin**
uk

**work description**
unpublished web site for a problem page

Given that you used a condom, it's unlikely that you are pregnant, although you could have a pregnancy test to reassure yourself. I think you're worrying about this because imagining this boy's baby inside you keeps you connected to him. Not only did this boy lie and use you for sex, he's made it clear he has no further interest in you. It's time you left him and found someone who really cares about you.

First, find out what the problem is - your shoes or your feet. Non leather shoes smell if they get wet. Wash your feet thoroughly and regularly. The most common cause of smelly feet is athletes foot. This is an infection which starts between the toes. Try anti fungal cream. Also, wear natural fibre socks and leather shoes.

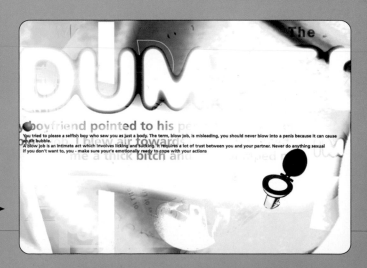

You tried to please a selfish boy who saw you as just a body. The term, blow job, is misleading, you should never blow into a penis because it can cause an air bubble.
A blow job is an intimate act which involves licking and sucking. It requires a lot of trust between you and your partner. Never do anything sexual if you don't want to, you - make sure you're emotionally ready to cope with your actions

## Contests

**Win these and other valuable prizes!**

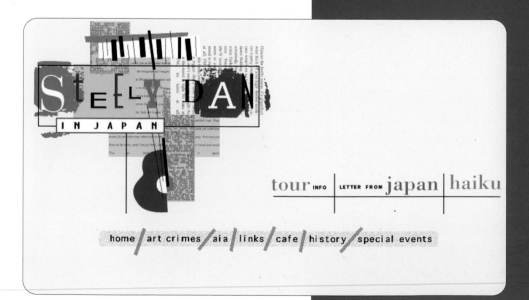

STEELY DAN
IN JAPAN

tour INFO | LETTER FROM japan | haiku

home / art crimes / aia | links / cafe | history / special events

UNBELIEVABLE !  AWESOME !  STUPENDOUS !

FABULOUS !  AMAZING !

*Special Events*

chats | contests

home / art crimes / aia / links / cafe / history / special events

**title**
steely dan web site

**address**
www.steelydan.com/

**client**
steely dan

**number of pages**
30

**design**
carol bobolts

**design company**
red herring design

**illustration**
carol bobolts, adam chiu, donald fagen

**programming**
jack mason, john limpert,
walter becker, gautam guiliani

**software**
bbedit, debabelizer,
photostat, real audio

**origin**
usa

**work description**
information web site with band
news and events

97.3

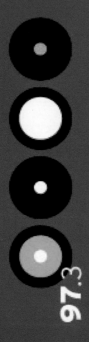

Web-Publishing

Konzept | Projekte | mail

Eitel > Technische Visualisierung

Konzept | Projekte | mail

agil > Visuelle Kommunikation

Konzept | Projekte | mail

WYSIWYG

**title**
agil-technische visualisierung

**address**
www.agil.de

**client**
agil, visuelle kommunikation
pforzheim & technische visualisierung.
andreas eitel

**number of pages**
26

**design**
peter kraus, andreas ochs

**design company**
agil. visuelle kommunikation

**programming**
andreas eitel

**software**
photoshop

**origin**
germany

**work description**
promotional web site for graphic
studios which develop and design
internet publications

**agil > Visuelle Kommunikation**

Konzept | Projekte | home

**agil** Visuelle Kommunikation
Kallhardtstraße 10
D-75173 Pforzheim

T    07231 / 9271-54/55
F    07231 / 9271-56
ISDN  07231 / 9271-57
Email  agil@kraus.pf.eunet.de

# www.dfuse.com

### WELCOME

hosting AMID Association of Music Industry Designers

**title**
d-fuse

**address**
www.dfuse.com

**number of pages**
250

**art direction**
michael faulkner, stuart gill

**design**
michael faulkner

**design company**
d-fuse/rawpawgraphics

**programming**
stuart gill, ian masters

**software**
bbedit, flash, freehand, photoshop

**origin**
uk

81

**work description**
promotional site for a web design group. the site is also home to a community of underground music labels, video artists, photographers, and graphic designers

SURFER'S PARADISE

press centre • urban high • archives • prague • bands •

**title**
boardx

**address**
www.boardx.com

**client**
richmond towers/ballantlne's

**number of pages**
20

**design**
rick nath

**design company**
noho digital

**software**
futuresplash

**origin**
uk

**work description**
web site promoting the urban high orbit
tent, linked to the world snowboarding
federation championships

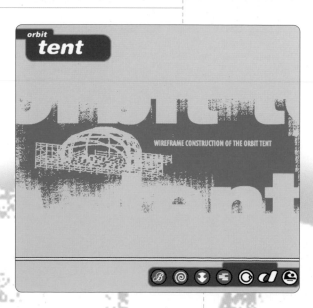

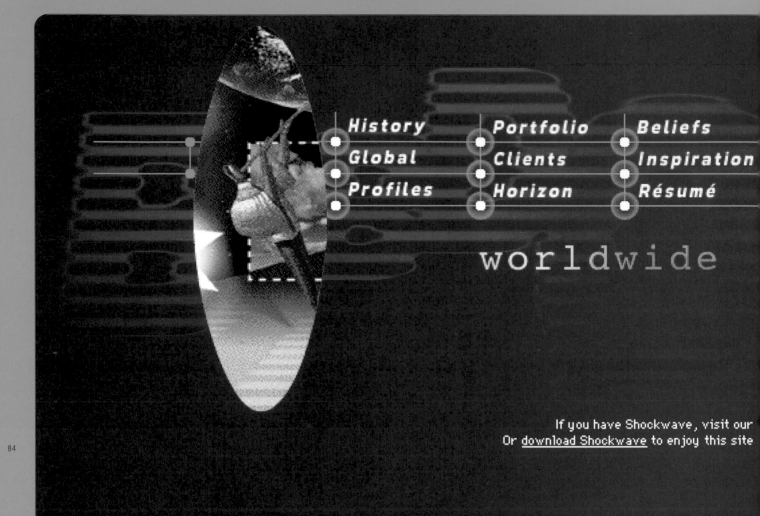

History       Portfolio      Beliefs
Global        Clients        Inspiration
Profiles      Horizon        Résumé

worldwide

If you have Shockwave, visit our
Or download Shockwave to enjoy this site

**work description**
promotional web site for an advertising
agency. text entries introduce different
topics and lead to "splash" screens,
which establish visual templates for the
editorial content of each section

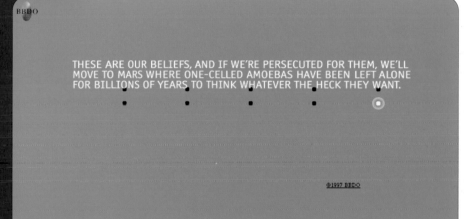

Credits

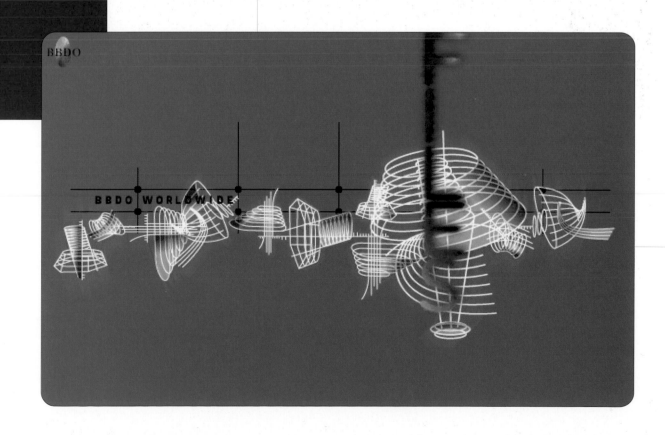

THESE ARE OUR BELIEFS, AND IF WE'RE PERSECUTED FOR THEM, WE'LL MOVE TO MARS WHERE ONE-CELLED AMOEBAS HAVE BEEN LEFT ALONE FOR BILLIONS OF YEARS TO THINK WHATEVER THE HECK THEY WANT.

©1997 BBDO

BBDO WORLDWIDE

**title**
bbdo worldwide web site

**address**
www.bbdo.com

**client**
bbdo

**number of pages**
85+

**art direction**
jennifer boyd, janine coover

**design**
whitney lowe, somi kim,
beth elliott, jens gehlhaar,
ken olling, scott fishkind

**design companies**
bbdo west, reverb, redant

**illustration**
jayme odgers, de ivett

**text**
david lubars, kathy hepinstall

**programming**
hillary safarik, chris sands

**software**
director, gifbuilder,
photoshop, simple text

**origin**
usa

85

*left*

**title**
razorfish

**address**
www.razorfish.com

**number of pages**
50

**design**
thomas mueller,
marc tinkler

**design company**
razorfish, inc.

**programming**
marc tinkler, oz lubling

**origin**
usa

**work description**
promotional web site for a design
company

*below and page 88*

**title**
the razorfish subnetwork

**address**
www.rsub.com

**number of pages**
100+

**art direction**
thomas mueller, craig kanarick,
peter mattei

**design**
thomas mueller

**design company**
razorfish, inc.

**programming**
craig kanarick, oz lubling,
marc tinkler, stephen turbek,
juliet martin

**origin**
usa

**work description**
information, education, and entertainment
web site

# the sub
## razorfish subnetwork
### the subnetwork

[ art, photography, literature, phlogiston ]

**the Nvelope** · [ messages from the brink of the millenium ]

**the blue dot**

**bunko!** · [ games, man! games ]

**this girl** ·

**disinformation** · [ the subculture search engine ]

[ the adventures of me, age 24 1/2 ]

 **typoGRAPHIC** · [ a digital exploration of type ]

razorfish

razorfish

o | | | | | | h

subAbsolutworkk
razor.sub
[subject sub
subsub.sub rsub

the blue dot

[ art, photography, literature, pHlogiston ]

bunko! ○ [ games, man! games ]

typoGRAPHIC
[ a digital exploration of type ]

theNvelope ○ [ messages from the brink of the millenium ]

this_girl * — [ the adventures of me, age 24 1/2 ]

disinformation [g] [ the subculture search engine ] <<

About RSUB   info@rsub.com

*below*

**title**
typographic

**address**
www.rsub.com/typo.

**number of pages**
100s

**design**
alex smith, stephen turbek, ian anderson

**design company**
razorfish, inc.

**programming**
oz lubing, stephen turbek

**origin**
usa

**work description**
educational web site for the
exploration of digital typography

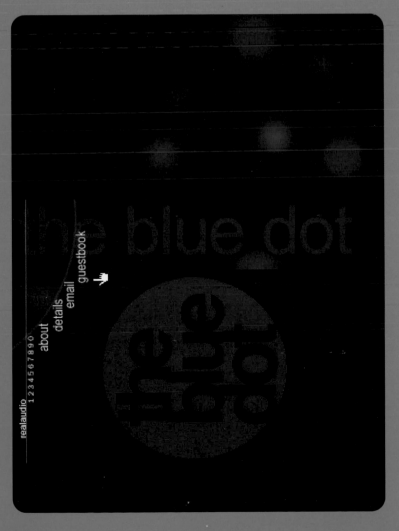

*above*

**title**
the blue dot

**address**
www.thebluedot.com

**number of pages**
100s

**design**
craig kanarick

**design company**
razorfish, inc.

**programming**
craig kanarick, oz lubling,
marc tinkler, stephen turbek,
juliet martin

**origin**
usa

**work description**
art and literature web site: one
of the first sites to use animations

90

# cd rom

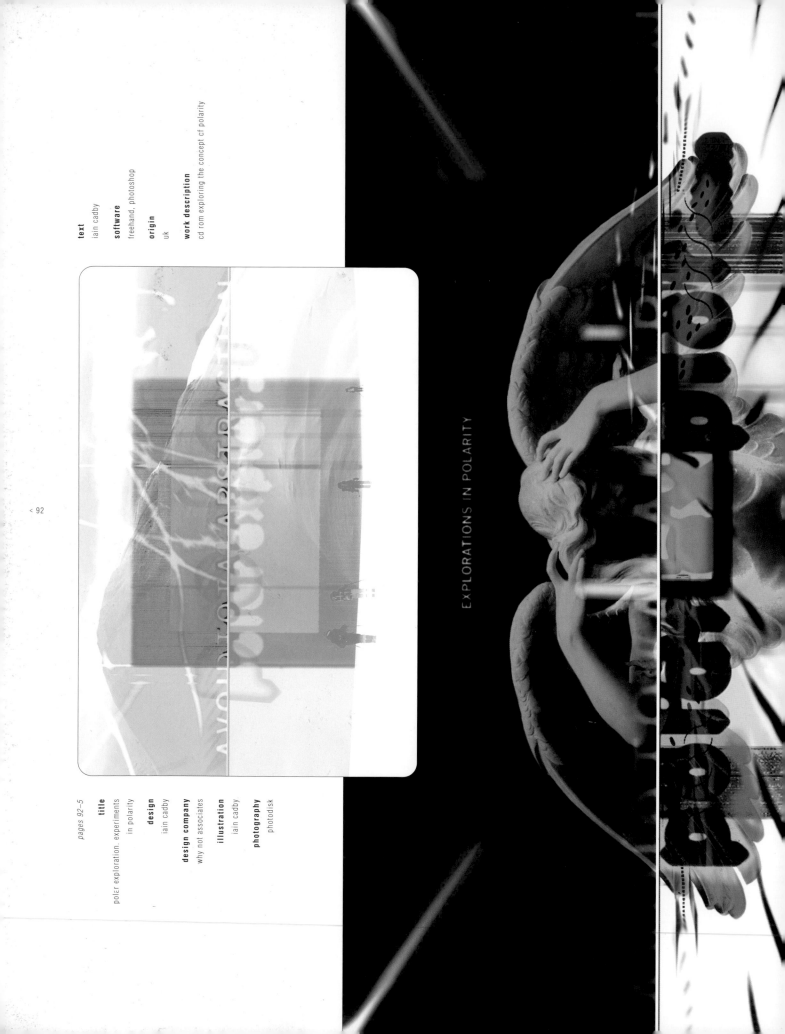

pages 92–5

**title**
polar exploration. experiments
in polarity

**design**
iain cadby

**design company**
why not associates

**illustration**
iain cadby

**photography**
photodisk

**text**
iain cadby

**software**
freehand, photoshop

**origin**
uk

**work description**
cd rom exploring the concept of polarity

EXPLORATIONS IN POLARITY

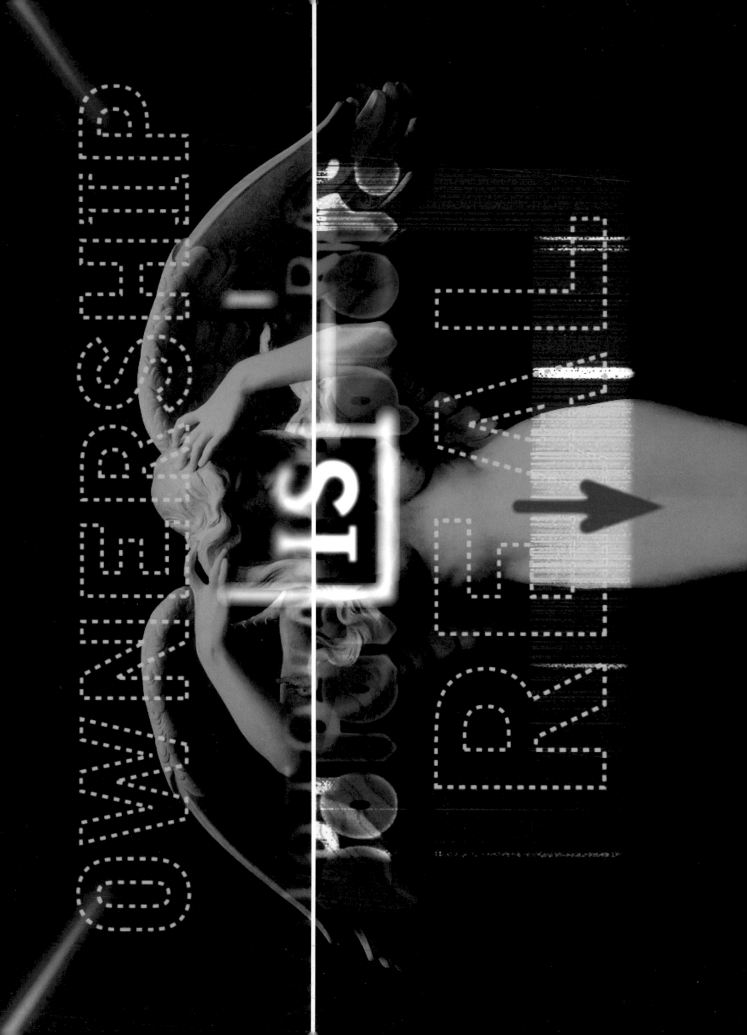

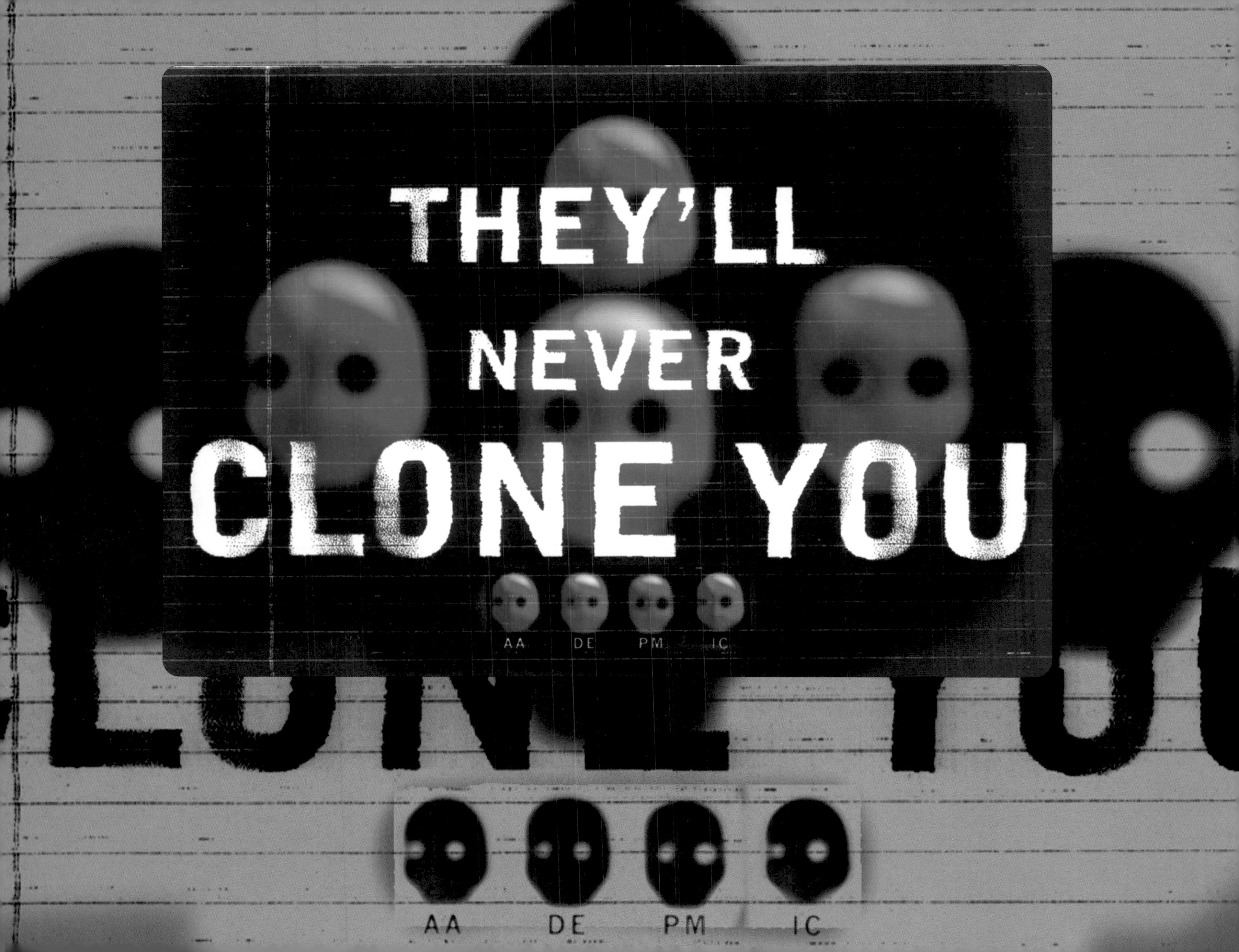

F 2

Alphab

Th

Beat

Screen Scream

*pages 96–9*

**title**
face2face no. 4

**client**
moniteurs, xplicit

**design**
alexander branczyk, stefan hauser,
thomas nagel, heike nehl,
alessio leonardo

**design companies**
moniteurs, xplicit

**photography**
tilman brems, frontpage photographers

**programming**
stefan hauser, andrea herstowski,
peter schmidt

**software**
director, fontographer, photoshop

**origin**
germany

**work description**
promotional cd rom containing eight
alphabets and three media performances

face

**habeat**

olicit ffm/Moniteurs

dtrack by Jammin' Unit, DJ Disko, General Magic

vk, elNag, haike, HausR, Leoló

Cilman et al

er Book

**SemiSerif**

GRID CAPS

**Madzine Script**

telle Sugo

BY DISRUPTING LEGIBILITY

*expressive*

TYPOGRAPHY CAN BE USED FOR ITS
FORMAL QUALITIES,
I.E. AS IMAGE,
IN BOTH PRINT
AND INTERACTIVE MEDIA.

The probability
is that digital
agents will be
personality
programmed
and will sift
information for
the reader
who will be
handed a.
concise
selected read
from a volume
of text.

It seems unlikely
that large amounts
of "book-like" text
will exist in
interactive media.

The digital agent will sift through data, for instance daily news,
and select information of specific interest
to the user.

*expressive*

Typography turns into typograms
by negation of its
legibility.

This is because
typography's hierarchy
creates a rhythm
INTO DIMENSIONS
it is a time based
at a certain speed

Apollinaire

concrete poetry

verbal, discussive model

more

The initial stage of this application
of linking devices and methods in
text

non-computer models

overt

literary theory

historical background

typography

additative authorship

origins of hypertext

re-construction of me

reader as author

is employed

Hypertext is used to form linking structures of non-linear text,

where visual and aural material, including

content links

this results in blocks of text becoming self-contained, less dependent
on the preceding and anteceding texts—in a very
simple way this embodies notions of post structuralist theory.

with *hypertext.*

formal links

humour

random meaning

pages 100–103

title
hypertype

address
www.alpertawards.com/typewriter

design
michael worthington

programming
michael worthington

software
after effects, director,
photoshop, typestry

origin
usa

work description
graduate thesis that logs the
possibilities for typography in
an interactive medium

*In print the way that you read is standardized.*

line....

IN

that they are next

IS A PROMPT

since their motion

TEXT IN INTERACTIVE MEDIA DOES NOT HAVE TO CONFORM SO STRICTLY TO THIS

WORDS

CAN JUMP IN FROM ANY

composition

SIDE

{size is everything}

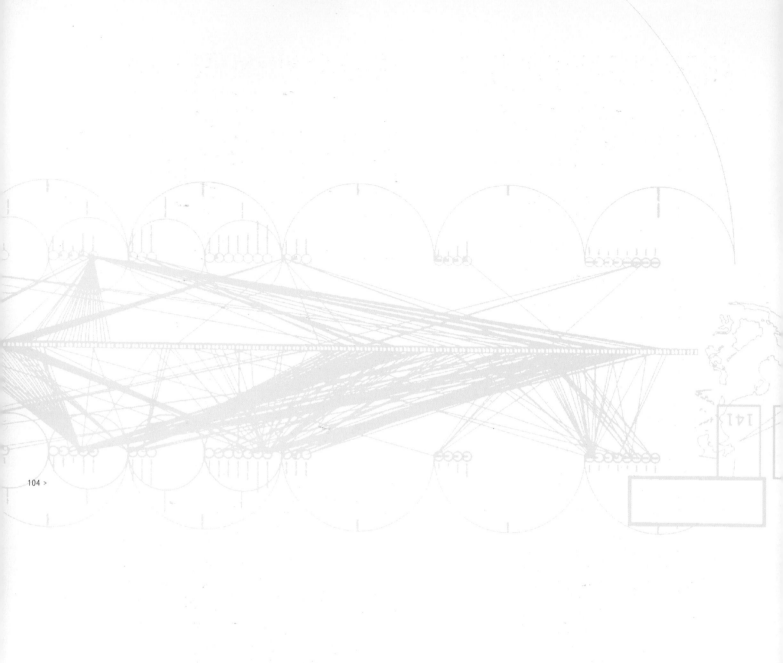

pages 104–7 (except page 107, right)

**title**
pagespace

**design**
philip o'dwyer

**programming**
philip o'dwyer

**software**
director

**origin**
uk

**work description**
unpublished study into the nature of
page-based information

The place of the study of communication in the history of science is neither trivial, fortuitous, nor new. Even before Newton such problems were current in physics, especially in the work of Fermat, Huygens, and Leibnitz, each of whom shared an interest in physics whose focus was not mechanics but optics, the communication of visual images.

# CHAPTER 1 CYBERNETICS IN HISTORY

Fermat furthered the study of optics with his principle of minimization which says that over any sufficiently short part of its course, light follows the path which it takes the least time to traverse. Huygens developed the primitive form of what is now known as Huygens' Principle by saying that light spreads from a source something like a small sphere consisting of secondary sources which in turn propagate light just as the primary sources do. Leibnitz, in the meantime, saw the whole world as a collection of beings called

A preoccupation with optics and with message, which is apparent in this part of Leibnitz's philosophy, runs through its whole texture. It plays a large part in two of his most original ideas: that of the Characteristica Universalis, or universal scientific language, and that of the Calculus Ratiocinator, imperfect calculus of logic. This Calculus Ratiocinator, imperfect as it was, was the direct of modern mathematical logic.

Leibnitz, dominated by ideas o
more than one way, the intelle
ideas of this book. For the very
machine computation and in au
book are very far from being u
problems with which I am conc
Leibnitzian. Leibnitz's computi
offshoot of his interest in a c
reasoning calculus which agai

optics

nature
navigation
neurology > brain, feedback
Newton, Issac
Newtonian physics
optics
optimization
output
pattern
photoelectric cells
probability
relativity, theory of
sense organs
taping

music box
message > cybernetics, communication, information
missiles, guided
monitors in automatic machinery > automata

non-linear filmmaking

analogue-digital conversion

...ssage, which is Leibnitz, dominated by ideas of communication, is, in more than one way, the intellectual ancestor of the ...sophy, runs clerk Maxwell and of his precursor, Faraday, and ...ideas of this book. for ba... also interested in attracted the attention of physicists once more

Toward the middle of the last century, the work

...Leibnitz's computing machines were only on ...of most of his interest in a computing language, a ...reasoning calculus which again was in his mind, merely ...an extension of his idea of a complete artificial ...language. Thus, even in his computing machine, ...Leibnitz's preoccupations were mostly linguistic and ...communicational

...was supposed to ...permeate the atmosphere, interstellar space and ...transparent materials. Clerk Maxwell's work on ...consisted in the mathematical development of id ...which had been previously expressed in a cogent ...non-mathematical form by Faraday. The study of

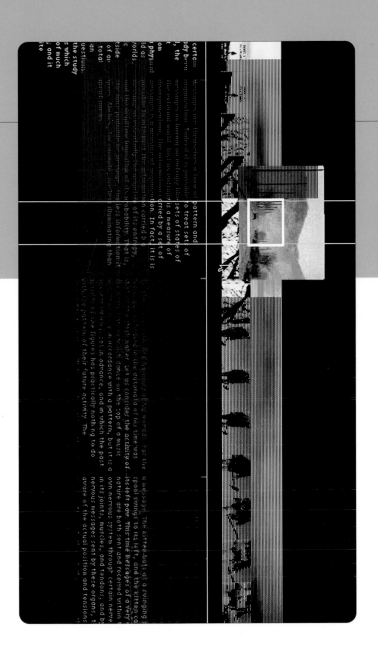

*right*

**title**
onedotzero stripspace

**client**
digilar/*creative review* magazine

**design**
mark breslin, philip o'dwyer

**design company**
lab

**programming**
philip o'dwyer

**software**
director, premiere

**origin**
uk

**work description**
promotional cd rom to accompany
the inaugural event of onedotzero, a
digital film festival at the ica, london.
the interface is based on a filmstrip
structure and integrated with layered
contextual information

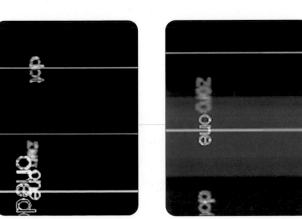
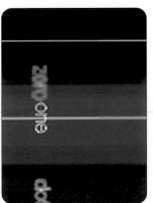
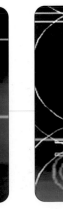
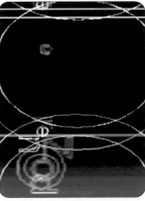

THE

THE

T tache OF

T tache OF tongue and thigh

It is leviathan and we

two
BY

**title**
the ache of marriage

**client**
dr jo berryman, calarts

**design**
david harlan

**text**
denise levertov

**software**
director, photoshop, sound edit

**origin**
usa

**work description**
a typographic manipulation of a poem

IN
THE
ARK
OF
THE
aCHE
OF
IT

KATSUHIKO HIBINO

112

工は積木によってつまれる事にあり、
型になるのが大事

"S" shall bring good luck in gambling
by shooting an arrow into the middle.

**title**
f omni

**client**
fuse 13 "superstition"

**design**
hibino

**publishers**
fontshop international

**work description**
digital typeface

113

**CONTEXTS STRUCT**

**CONTEXTS STRUCT**

114

In a fully **denatured** interactive environment

Context becomes denatured when
it is possible to represent any
element in a context arbitrorily removed from its original use and
combined with another context
equally far removed from its original use.

CO

**title**
3°

**design**
weston bingham

**programming**
weston bingham

**software**
director, photoshop, illustrator

**origin**
usa

**work description**
graduate thesis exploring the interwoven
form, structure, and content of a screen-
based digital environment

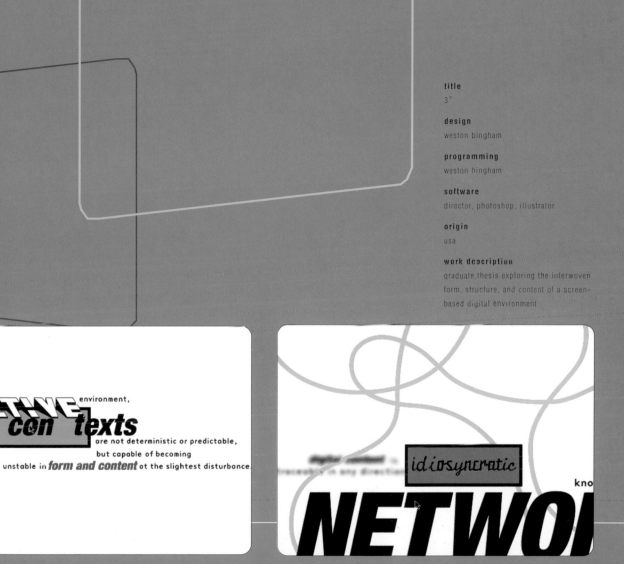

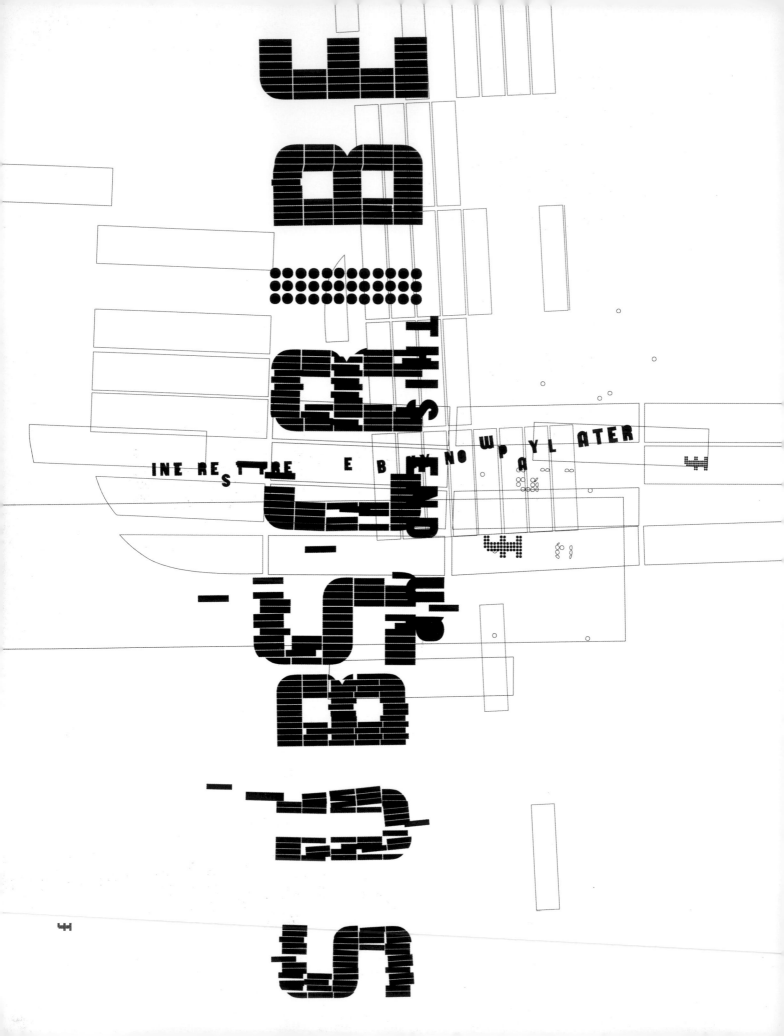

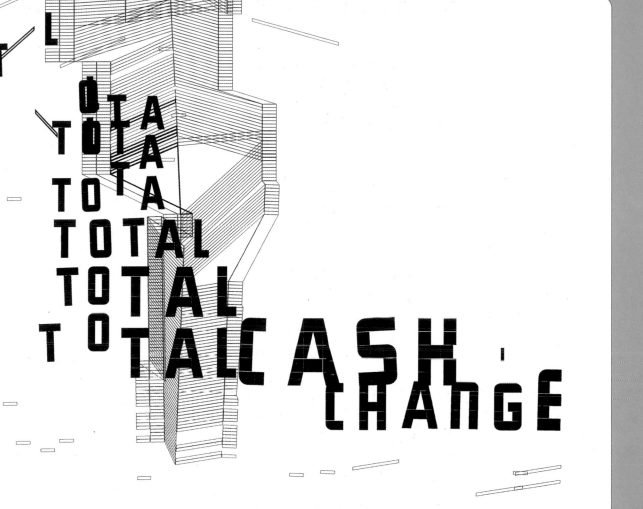

TOTAL CASH CHANGE

**title**
space as god

**client**
iso/glasgow jazz festival

**design**
mark breslin

**software**
director, fontographer, freehand

**origin**
uk

**work description**
unpublished artwork providing a visual
backdrop for an annual club/jazz event

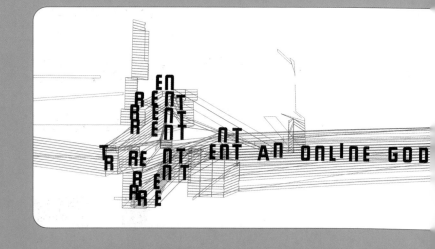

RENT AN ONLINE GOD

title
thickface records

client
segura inc.

number of pages
5

design
jason reeves

design company
pipe design

photography
carlos segura

programming
jason reeves

software
director, photoshop

origin
usa

work description
promotional interactive cd rom
for a record label

**title**
shorthandlite

**design**
jonathan hitchen

**design company**
beaufonts

**programming**
jonathan hitchen

**software**
director

**origin**
uk

**work description**
promotional cd rom that allows the user
to create and view symbols

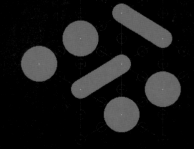

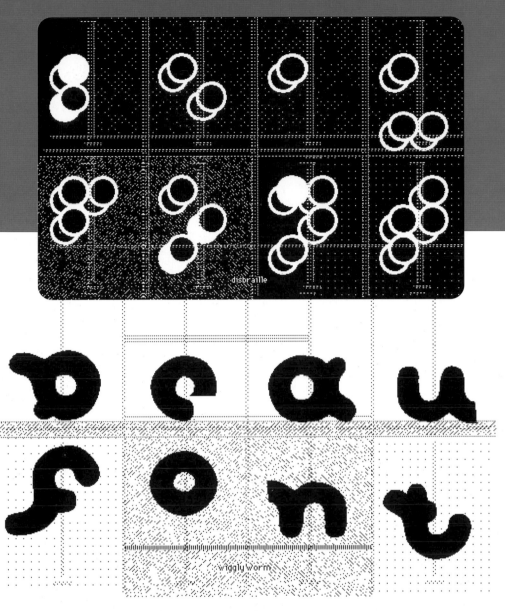

disbraille

wiggly worm

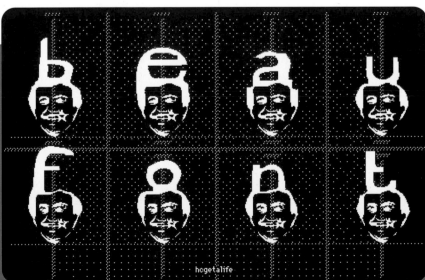

hcgetalife

**title**
excess baggage/viewfonts

**art direction**
jonathan hitchen

**design company**
beaufonts

**programming**
jonathan hitchen

**software**
hypercard

**origin**
uk

**work description**
promotional on-screen font
demonstration

121

**title**
header: 1

**client**
header

**design**
tom hingston

**design company**
tom hingston

**programming**
martin aberdeen

**software**
director

**origin**
uk

**work description**
interactive audio cd rom project with a
sequence taken from a record label's
back catalog

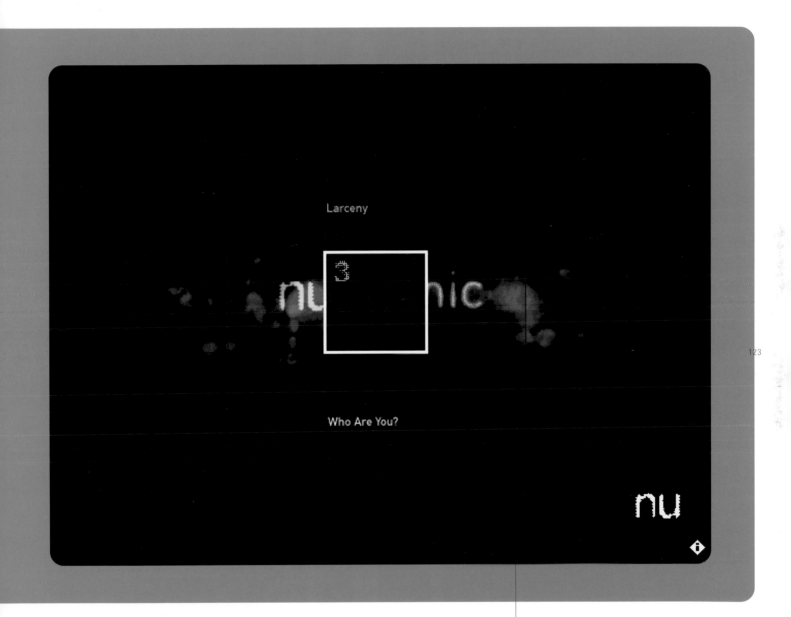

Day on

Just
receive
a phon
call.
Have a
meetin
at
14.00.
253
Centra
Park
West.

Day one He hands me a photograph the address and the usual amount. Fuck, how can this happen? One digital glitch and you're a dead man. Day two Bought the ticket. On my way to Europe, London. I'll kill the pig! The pain returns to my head.

Another Job. The client tells me that he misplaced an e.mail; need to kill the receiver. He hands me a photograph, the e.mail address and the usual amount. Still, one can not leave a trace ...

No trace

**title**
doppelgänger – the black issue

**design**
christian küsters, lorenzo suau-mercer

**design company**
doppelgänger

**programming**
david loosmore

**software**
director, photoshop, premiere, sound edit

**origin**
uk

**work description**
experimental graphic novel exploring the narrative structure of storytelling in the digital realm

# BLUTOPIA

indigo

jazz

ambienceman

CLICK
(his)

funking
head in

drum

deepbluedream

quit

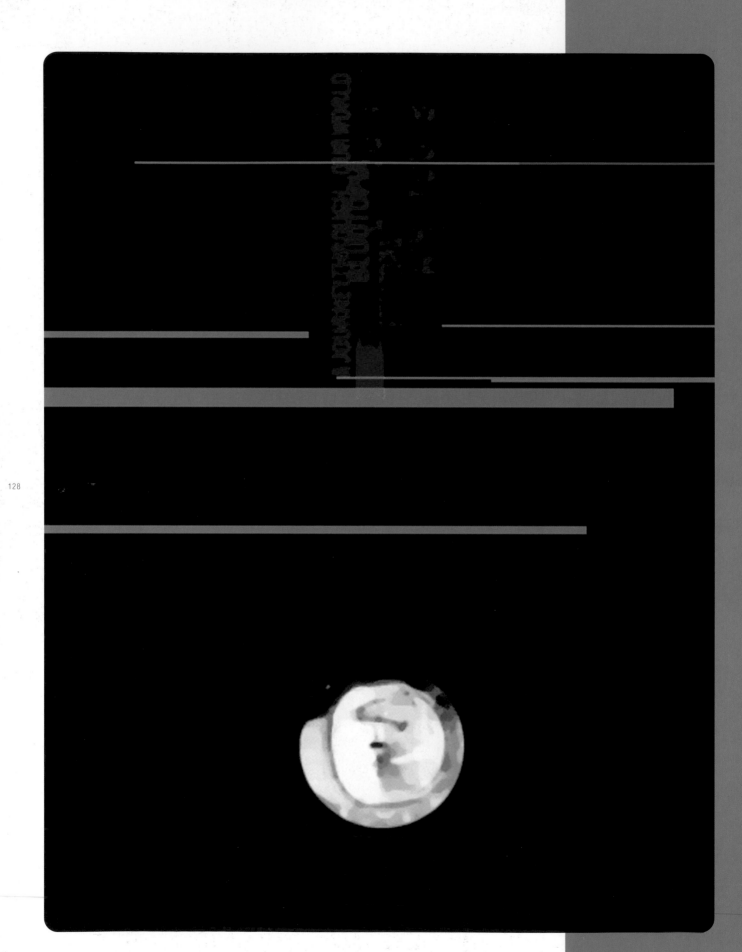

128

pages 126–9

**title**
blutopia – a journey through our world

**art direction**
dan witchell, nima talatoori

**design**
dan witchell

**design company**
blutopia

**software**
director, fontographer, photoshop

**origin**
uk

**work description**
promotional cd rom for a
design company

**title**
a tomato project

**art direction**
tomato

**design**
tomato/anti rom

**design company**
tomato

**programming**
anti rom

**software**
director

**origin**
uk

**work description**
unpublished interactive portfolio

**A TOMATO PROJECT**

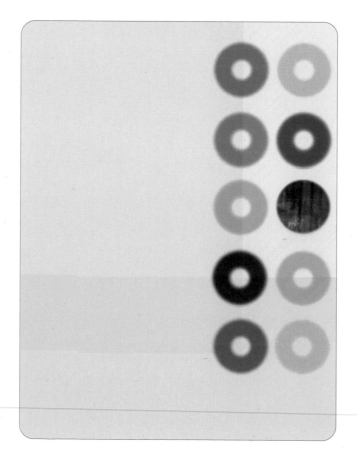

rage hides the f ear in our h earts

**title**
audiorom beta 1

**art direction**
mike bennett

**design**
mike bennett, chris penny,
paul hopton, andre ktori

**design company**
sunbather

**illustration**
mike bennett

**programming**
chris penny, paul hopton,
andre ktori

**software**
director, freehand,
photoshop

**origin**
uk

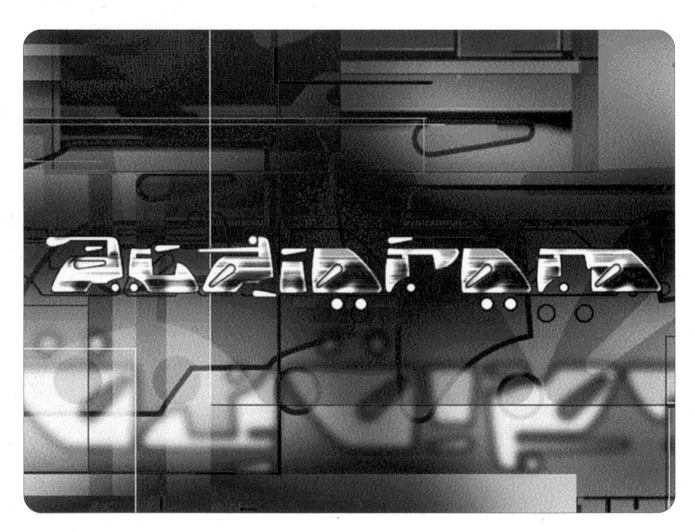

**work description**
enhanced promotional cd rom which
functions as an audio cd with three
tracks of original music and various
music "toys"

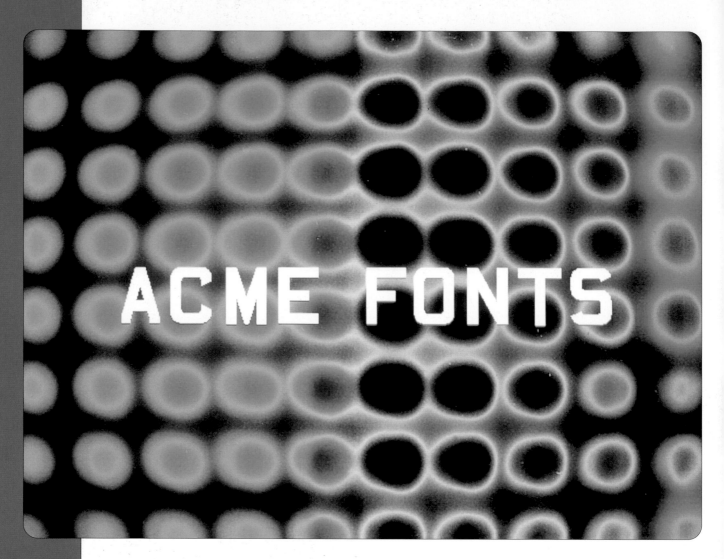

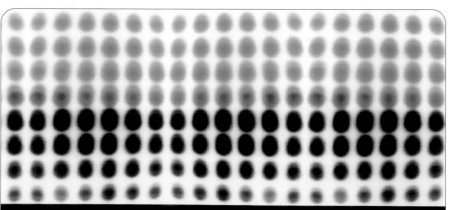

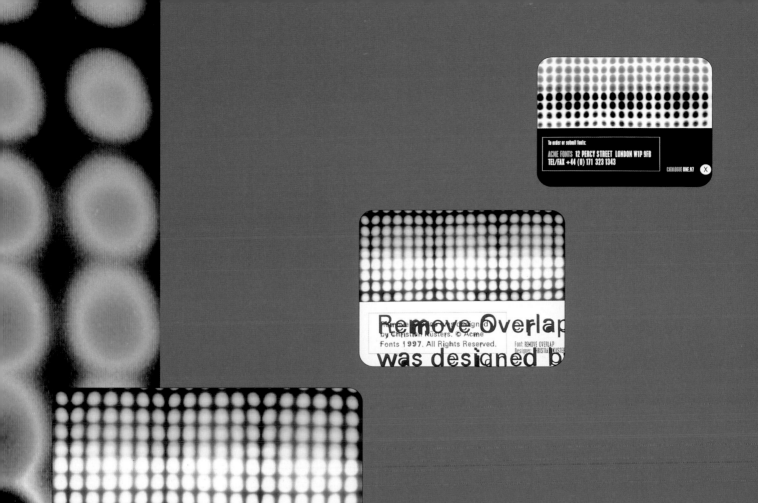

Remove Overlap

was designed b

Font: REMOVE OVERLAP
Designer: CHRISTIAN KUSTERS

Remove Overlap (was designed)
by Christian Kusters. © Acme
Fonts 1997. All Rights Reserved.

Font: HADRIAN
Designer: CHRISTIAN KUSTERS

137

**title**
acme fonts catalogue, one, 97

**client**
acme fonts

**design**
christian küsters

**design company**
chk design ltd

**photography**
paul wesley griggs

**programming**
david loosmore

**software**
director, photoshop

**origin**
uk

**work description**
cd rom catalog for a digital
typefoundry, which acts as a forum
for the presentation and discussion
of new typefaces

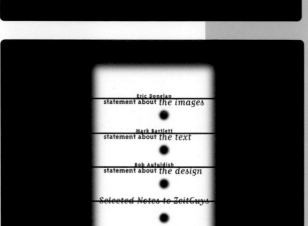

138

*above*

**title**
selected notes 2 zeitguys

**client**
*zed* journal

**design**
bob aufuldish

**design company**
aufuldish & warinner

**illustration**
eric donelan (donelan design)
bob aufuldish

**text**
mark bartlett

**programming**
david karam (post tool design)
bob aufuldish

**software**
director, illustrator, photoshop,
sound edit

**origin**
usa

**work description**
collaborative cd rom with a "pop-up"
interface connecting zeitguys, a
collection of 126 illustrations in font
format. by moving the cursor around
the blurred screen, areas of the page
come into focus

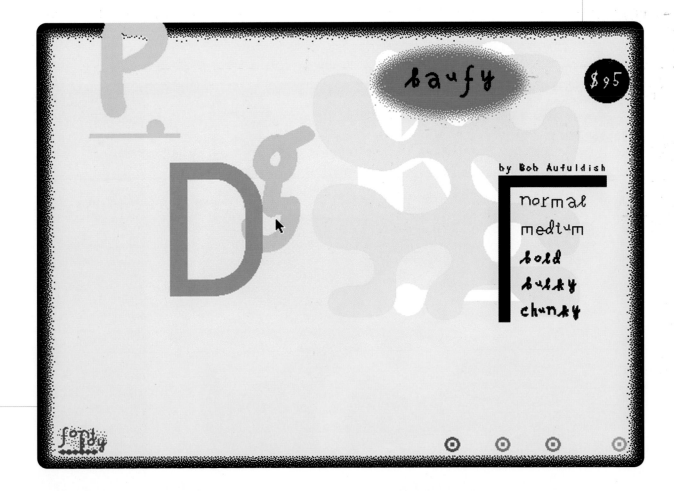

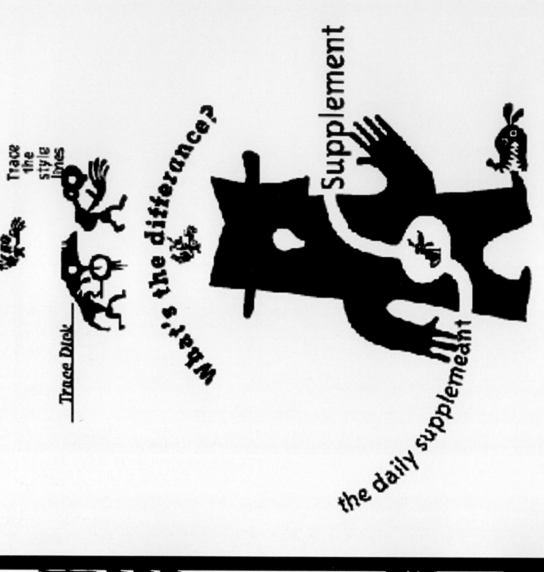

**title**
fontboy web site

**address**
www.well.com/~bobauf/fontboy.html

**client**
fontboy

**number of pages**
30

**design**
bob aufuldish

**design company**
aufuldish & warinner

**programming**
bob aufuldish

**software**
illustrator, photoshop

**origin**
usa

**work description**
promotional web site for a font library.
extracts from an essay by mark bartlett,
"beyond the margins of the page", put the
fonts in their cultural/theoretical context

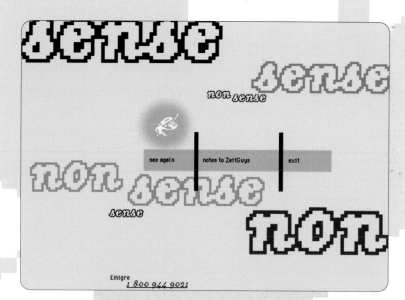

141

*left and right*

**title**
zeitmovie

**client**
emigre

**design**
bob aufuldish

**design company**
aufuldish & warinner

**illustration**
eric donelan (donelan design)
bob aufuldish

**programming**
bob aufuldish

**software**
director, illustrator,
photoshop, sound edit

**origin**
usa

**work description**
interactive promotional
presentation for zeitguys, 126
illustrations in font format

*Une coproduction : Réunion des musées nationaux, Télérama et index+*

# Moi, Paul Cézanne

*Auteurs : Olivier Cena, François Granon, Laurent Boudier*
*Réalisateurs : Emmanuel Olivier, Vincent Berlioz*

*Les textes, écrits par les auteurs, sont inspirés*
*de la correspondance de Paul Cézanne et de propos qui lui furent prêtés.*

**Télérama**  **Réunion des Musées Nationaux**  **index+**

Les lieux

 l'atelier

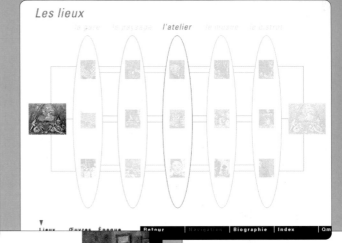

Lieux Œuvres Époque | Retour | Navigation | Biographie | Index | Qm

Jean-Louis Forain (1852-1931)

Peintre, graveur et caricaturiste,
Forain fit partie, malgré son jeune
âge, du groupe impressionniste.
Ami de Degas et de Huysmans,
Forain épatait ses aînés par
sa facilité. Après l'avoir vu copier
un Chardin au Louvre, Cézanne
raconta son admiration à Vollard:
«Le bougre, dit-il, savait déjà
indiquer le pli d'un vêtement»,
peut-être est-ce pour cela
qu'il possédait, dans son atelier,
plusieurs dessins satiriques
de Forain. Mais le bohème rebelle
et barbu deviendra en vieillissant
- et malgré son goût pour
la caricature et l'ironie -
un artiste rangé ayant fait fortune
dans le dessin de presse.
Sa peinture en souffrira, mais non
sa carrière: il finira sa vie membre
de l'Institut et président de la Société
nationale des beaux-arts.

| Retour | Navigation | Biographie | Index | Qm

*Biographie*

*Paul Céza...*

*1...*

| Retour | Navigation | Biograp...

**title**
moi, paul cézanne

**client**
rmn, télérama, index+

**art direction**
g. dairou

**design**
g. dairou, f. locca, e. mineur,
e. auger, a. dangeul

**design company**
index+

**photography**
t. cuisset, m. castro

**programming**
v. berlioz

**software**
director, illustrator, photoshop,
quickmove, zoom

**origin**
france

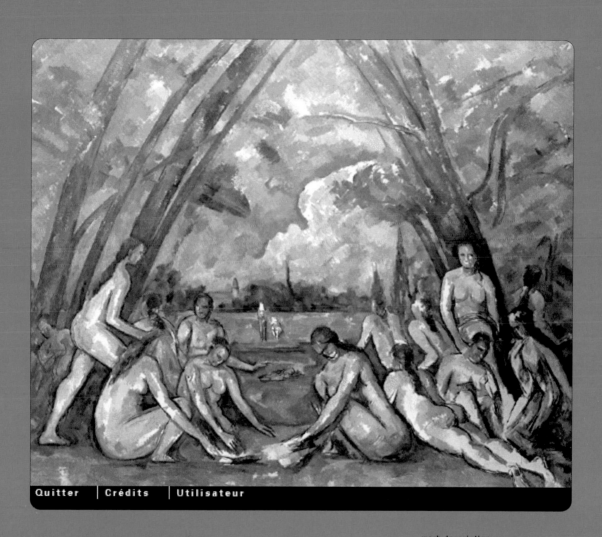

Quitter | Crédits | Utilisateur

143

**work description**
an exploration of the artist's
life and work

# Sommaire

< 144

1100  1200  1300  1400  1500  1600  1700  1800  1900

- Pyramide
- Richelieu
- Sully
- Denon

## Le Palais

## Les Collections

## Pyramide

● Le Hall Napoléon
● La transparence

Lieu

▼ Retour  Sommaire

## Région Richelieu

salle 38  Hollande, deuxième moitié du XVIIe siècle

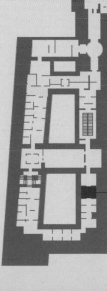

**La Dentellière**, 1665, Johannes Vermeer
École du nord - Hollande XVIe et XVIIe siècles

Salle

▼ Retour  Sommaire

**La Dentellière**, 1665
Johannes Vermeer 1632-1675, toile 0.24 × 0.21

Détails

Salle 38

▼ Retour  Sommaire

**title**
le louvre, peintures et palais

**client**
rmn, montparnasse multimédia

**art direction**
g. dairou

**design**
g. dairou, m. maffre, e. ucla, f. locca

**design company**
index+

**photography**
rmn, epgl, giraudon

**programming**
j.f. brouillet, c. coutard,
v. berlioz, j. b. delard

**software**
director, illustrator, photoshop

**origin**
france

**work description**
interactive visit to the louvre showing a selection
of 100 masterpieces

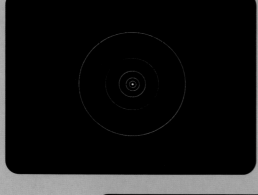

*pages 146–9*

**title**
national centre for popular music

**client**
music heritage ltd

**design**
dom raban, dave kirkwood

**design companies**
eg.g, guidance

**photography**
mark burden, andrew putler

**software**
director, illustrator, infini-d,
photoshop

**origin**
uk

**work description**
promotional cd rom for an exhibition
center devoted to the history and
development of popular music

# NATIONAL CENTRE FOR POPULAR MUSIC

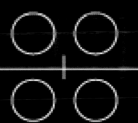

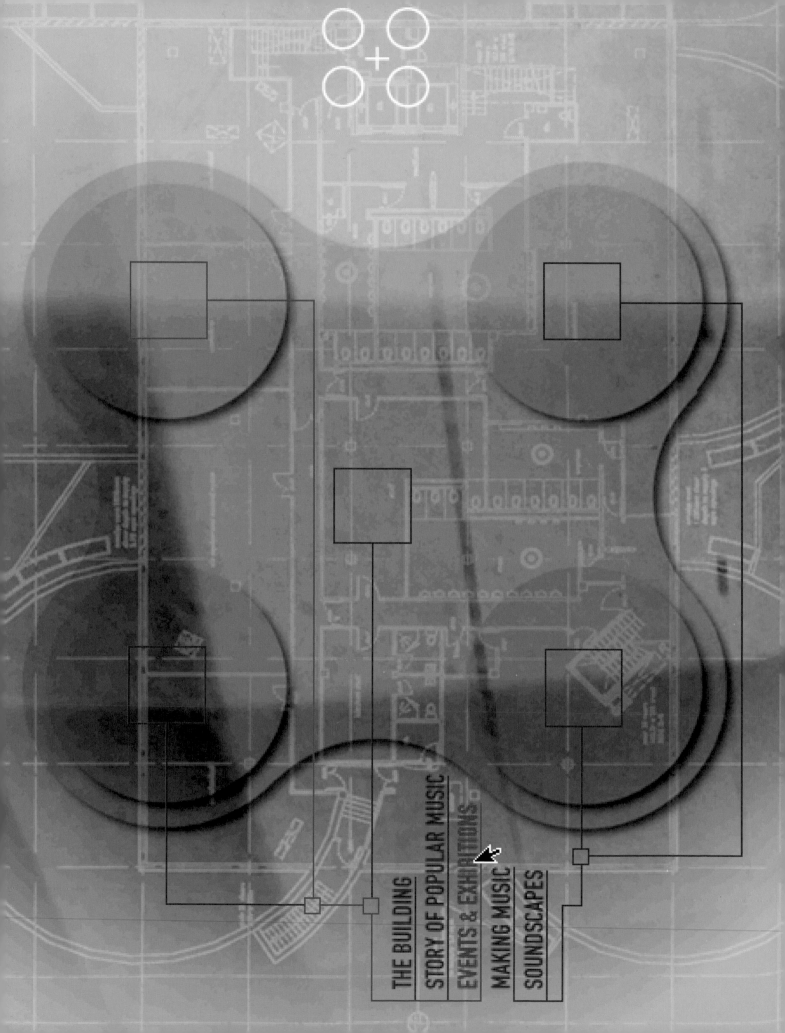

THE BUILDING

STORY OF POPULAR MUSIC

EVENTS & EXHIBITIONS

MAKING MUSIC

SOUNDSCAPES

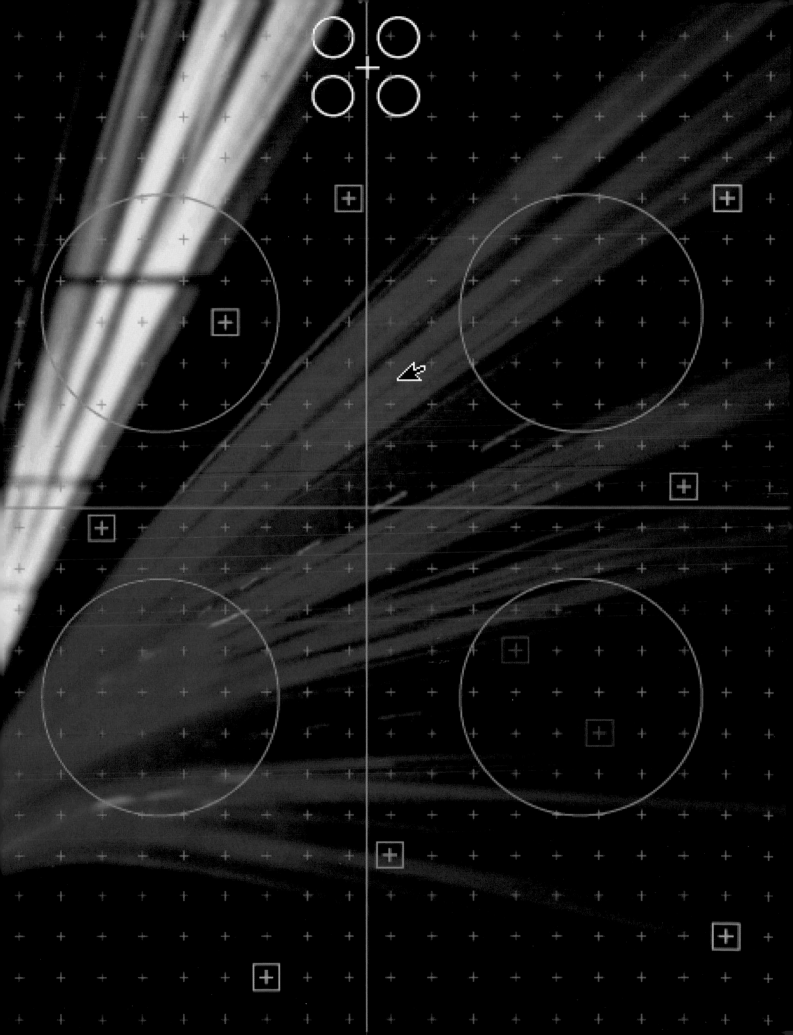

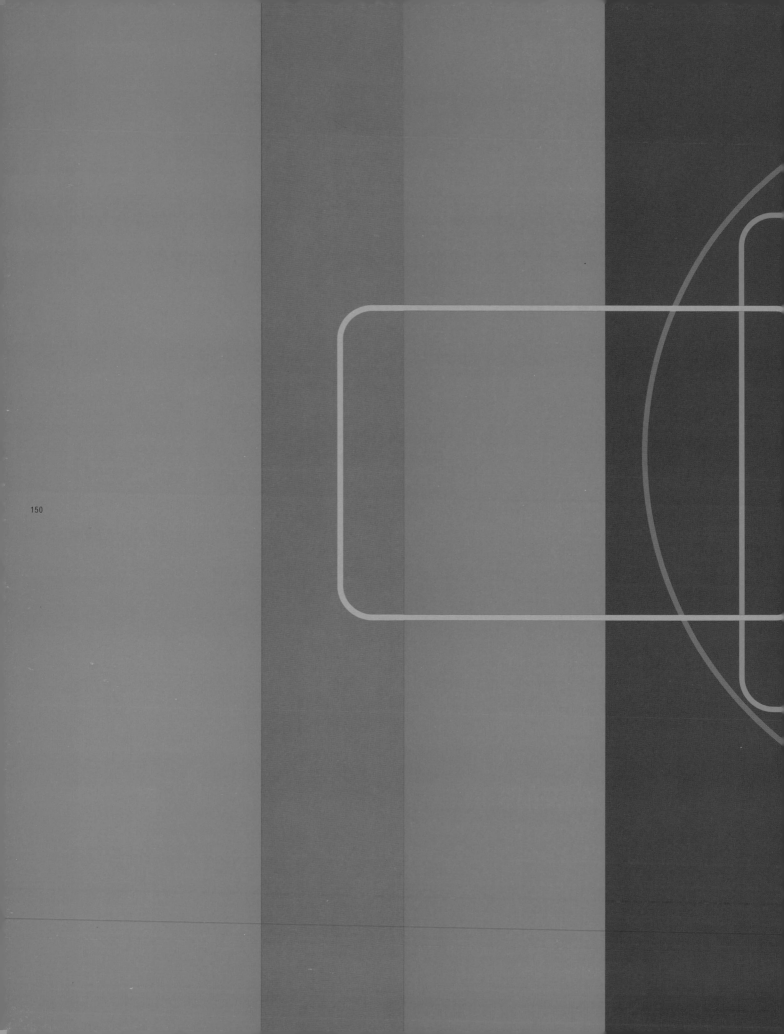

150

unpublished

COMMUNICATION

COMMUNICATION

connection

pages 152–5

**title**
graphic communication

**design**
pornchai doyle

**design company**
king prawn

**photography**
pornchai doyle

**programming**
dr bob

**software**
director

**origin**
uk

**work description**
experimental multimedia project

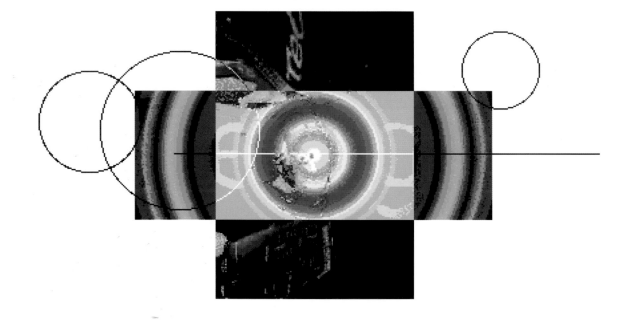

Inter
active

Design

IDEA

PROGRAM

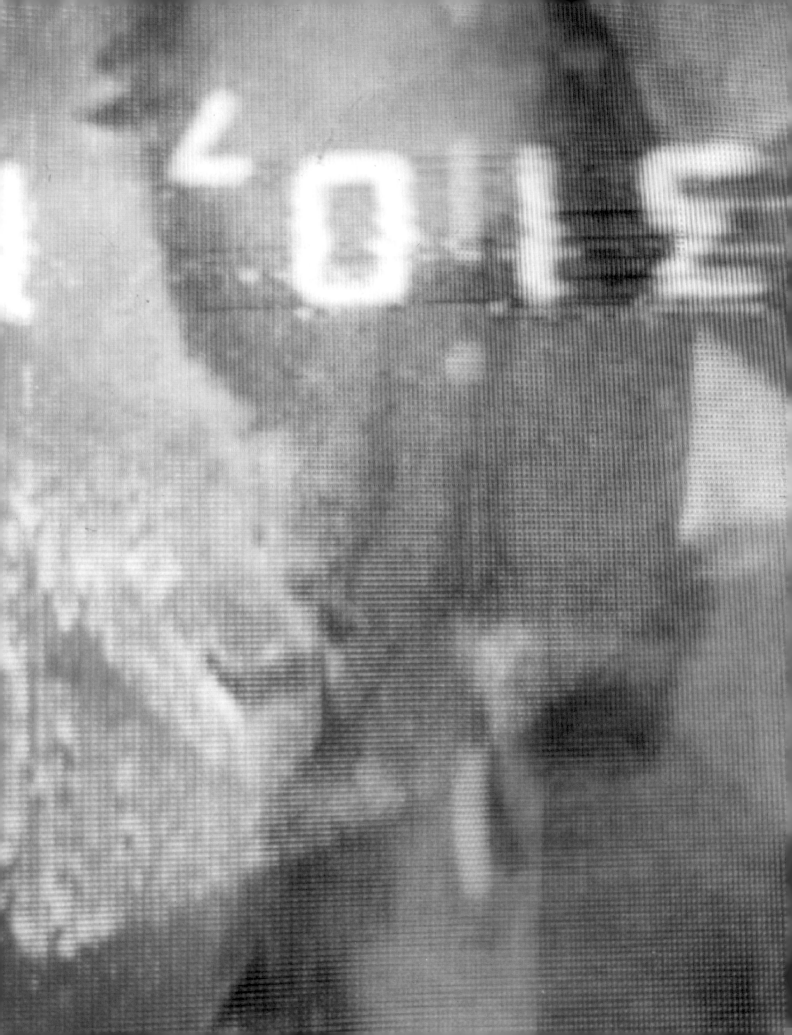

*pages 156–9*

**title**
hybrid animation a-z

**design**
darrell gibbons

**photography**
darrell gibbons

**software**
photoshop, quantel paintbox

**origin**
uk

**work description**

hybrid typefaces scanned, composed
"in camera", and animated to create new
typographic templates

*page 160–63*

**title**
visual and natural poetry

**design**
ainsley bowen

**software**
director, photoshop, sound edit

**origin**
uk

**work description**
typographic interpretation on film
of conversations overheard on the
streets of london and amsterdam

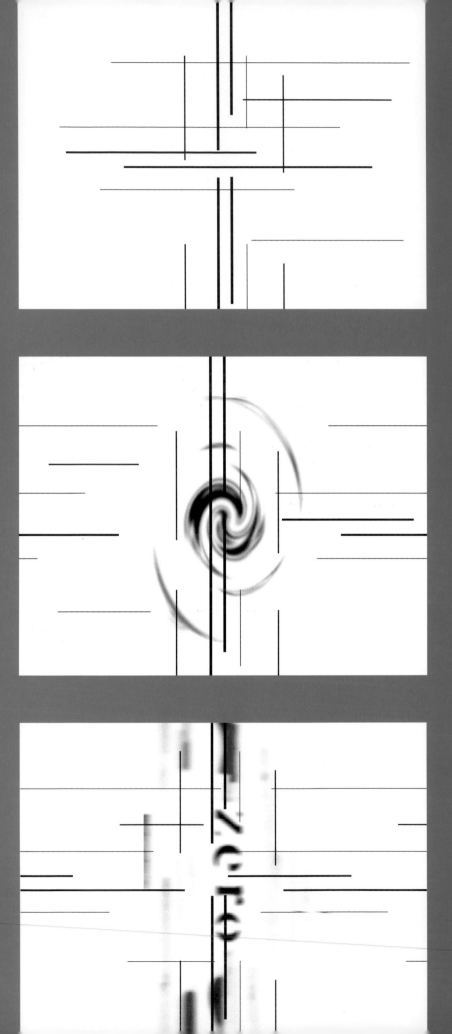

**title**
zero

**design**
michael loizides

**software**
director

**origin**
uk

**work description**
promotional animation clip for an
experimental magazine on
alternative culture

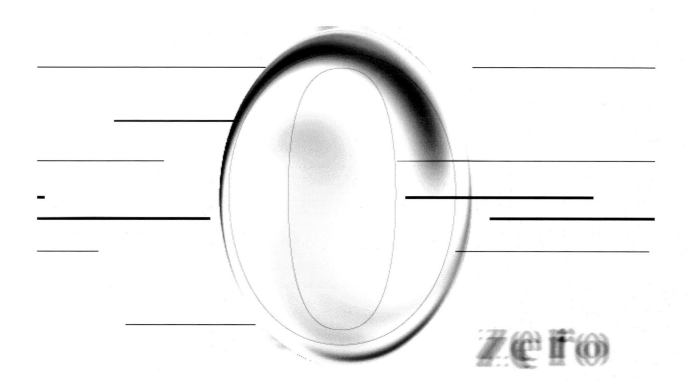

zero

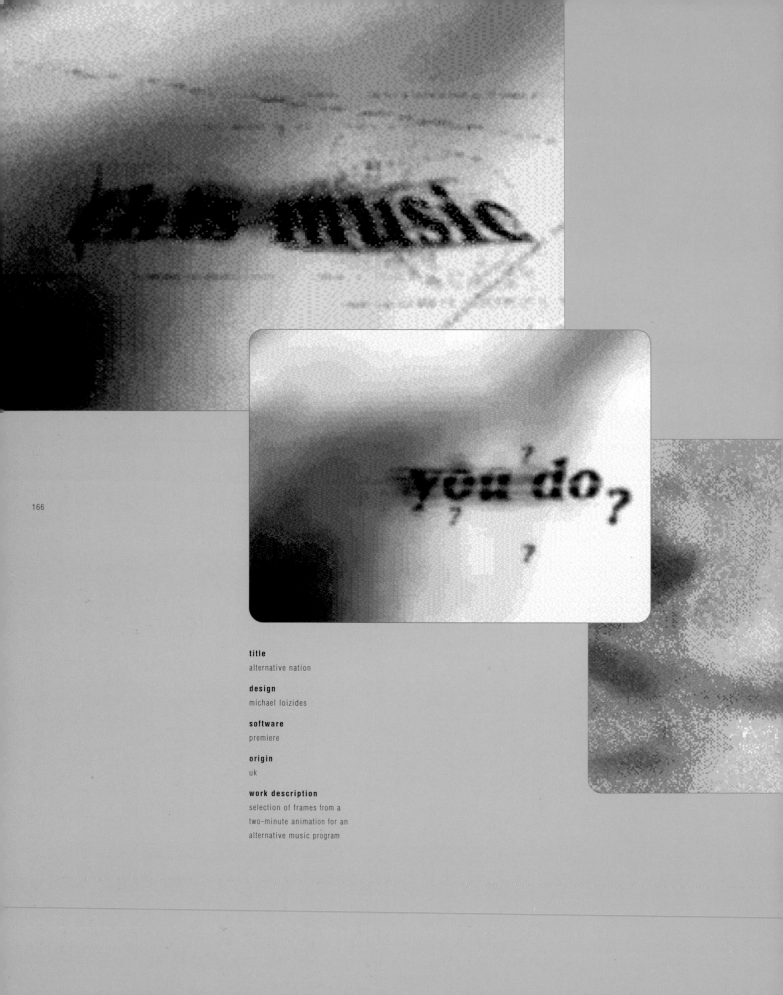

**title**
alternative nation

**design**
michael loizides

**software**
premiere

**origin**
uk

**work description**
selection of frames from a
two-minute animation for an
alternative music program

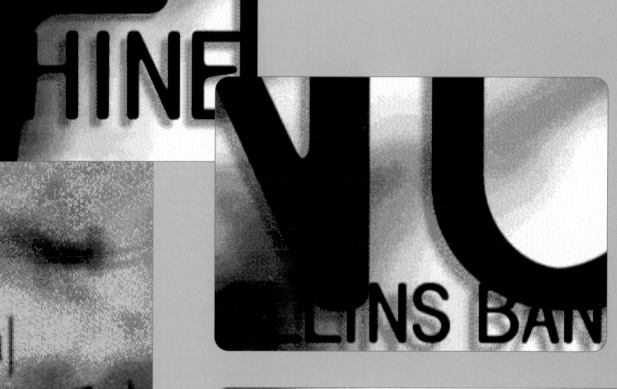

HINE

[uh]

uh

LINS BAN

Alternative
Nation

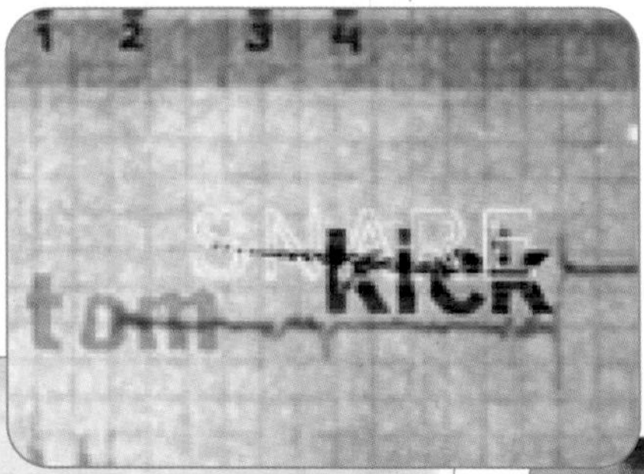

1 2 3 4

SNARE

tom kick

1 2 3 4

n iha

strings keyboard V

**title**
the visual representation of music

**design**
miranda may

**programming**
miranda may

**software**
director, infini-d,
photoshop, premiere

**origin**
uk

**work description**
stills from animations using typography
and abstract forms to attach visual
events to musical structures

**title**
visual representation of spoken language

**design**
garry waller

**illustration**
garry waller

**photography**
garry waller

**software**
premiere

**origin**
uk

**work description**
a series of short animations
representing spoken language
in typographic form

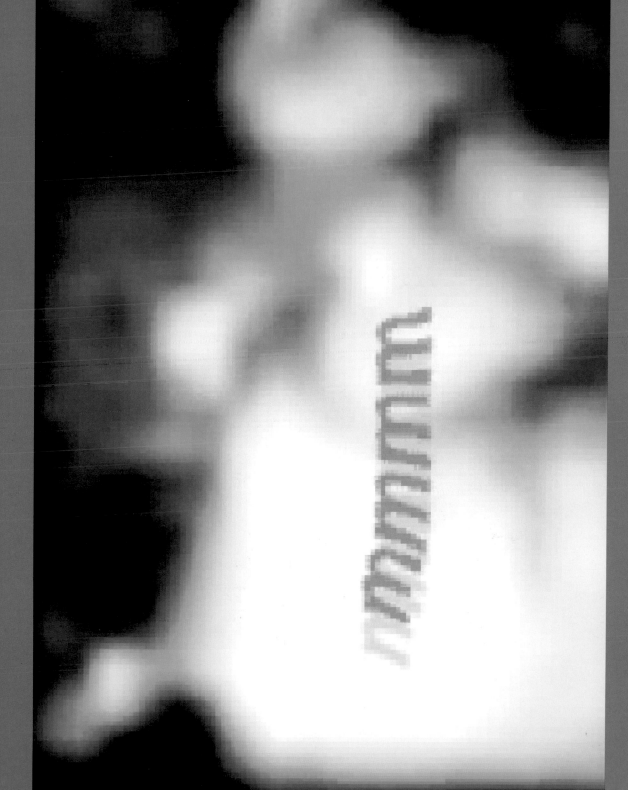

# Letters from London

This suitcase contains some of my personal letters which I wrote while I was in London.

They contain a lot of my ideas about the different things that are going on in the city, some bad, some good.

Since I came to London , I wrote a lot of letters to my friends back in Thailand.

And now, I'm on my way to the post office to send them. If you want to know some of the things I wrote just click on the black button of the suitecase to find out.

what're inside ?

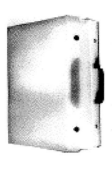

This suitecase have contain some of my

personal idea about
, what do i think about some kind of arts and artists
that we could find on the street of London.

pages 172–5

**title**
letters from london

**design**
m.l. varudh varavarn (win)

**illustration**
m.l. varudh varavarn (win)

**photography**
m.l. varudh varavarn (win)

**software**
director, photoshop, premiere

**origin**
uk

**work description**
experimental multimedia
project representing a foreign
visitor's impressions of
london in a series of letters

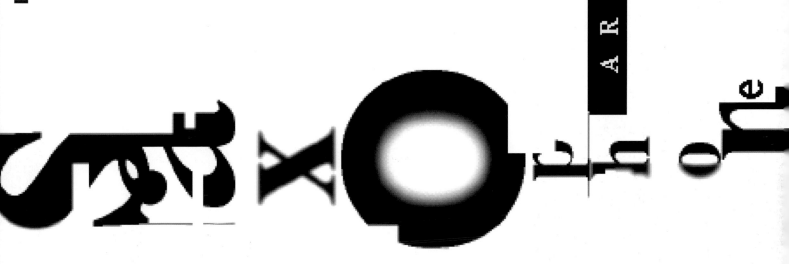

ARTIST

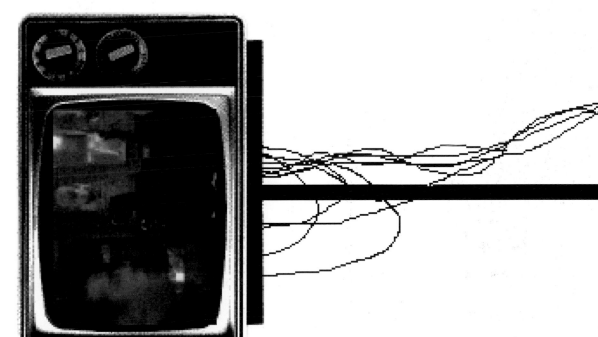

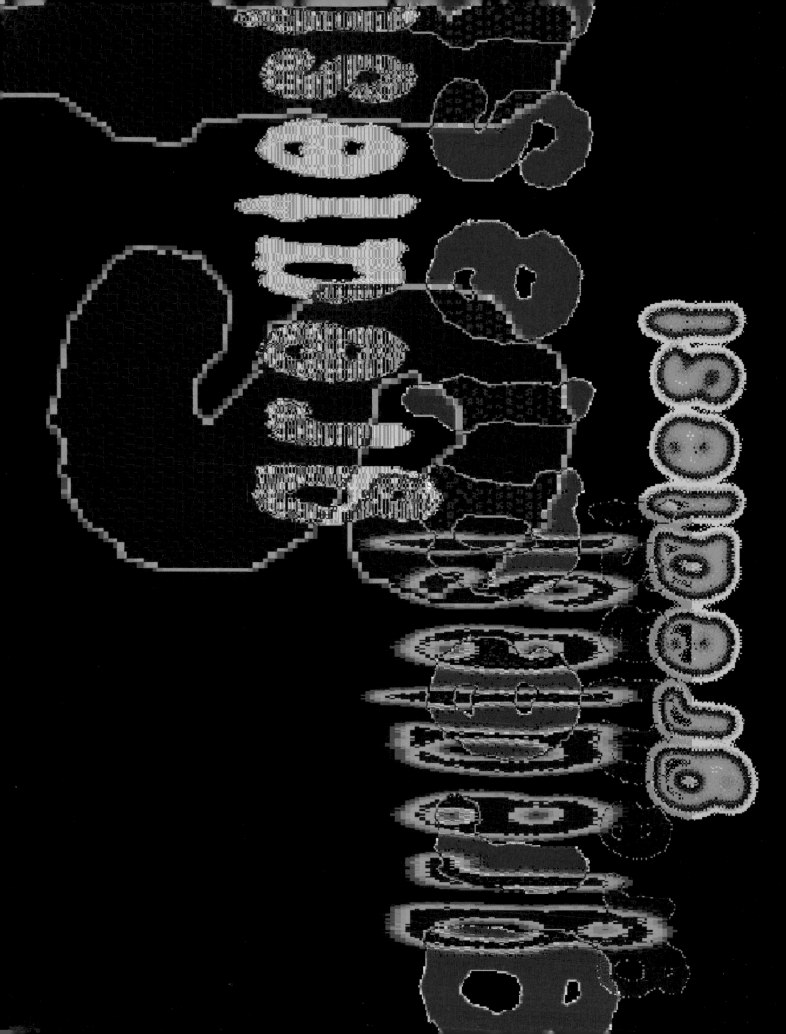

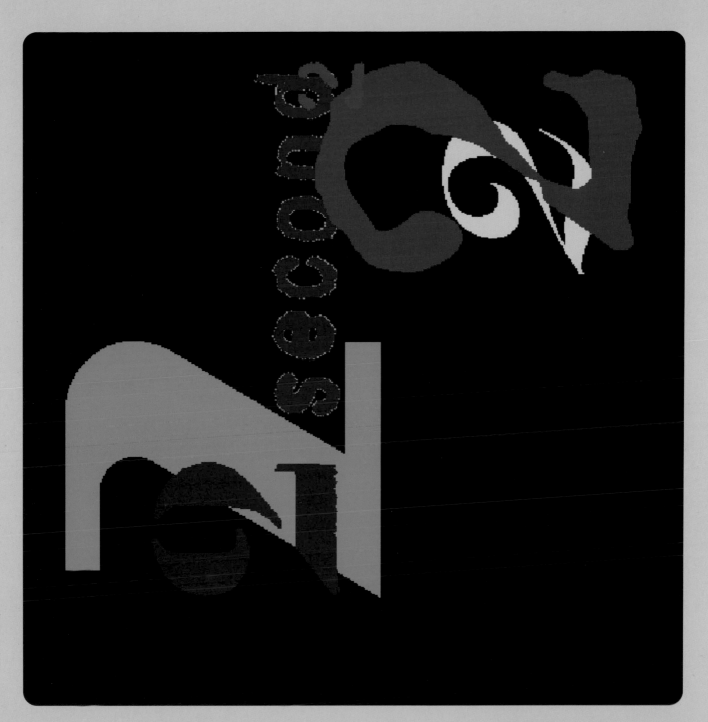

pages 176–9

**title**
colombian biodiversity

**client**
isabel gutiérrez

**design**
olga lucía holguín

**photography**
olga lucía holguín

**software**
director, photoshop, sound edit

**origin**
usa

**work description**
educational cd rom to raise public
awareness of the urgent need to
preserve colombia's vast, but
diminishing, biodiversity

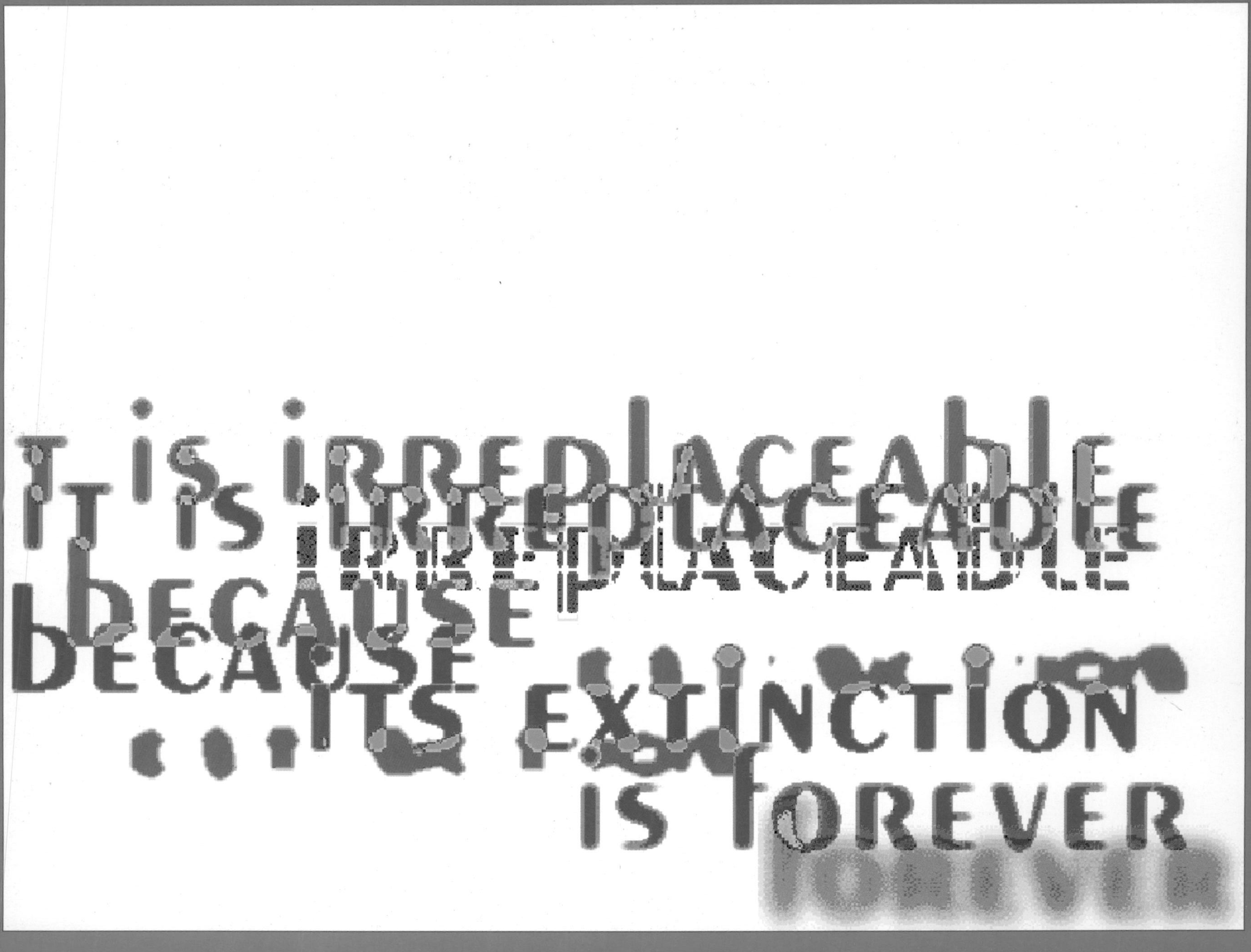

IT IS IRREPLACEABLE
BECAUSE EXTINCTION
IS FOREVER

The loss of biodiversity

180

**title**
internet project

**design**
sarah cromwell, nick whiting

**illustration**
sarah cromwell, nick whiting

**photography**
sarah cromwell, nick whiting

**software**
premiere

**origin**
uk

**work description**
experimental video inspired by the concept
of the internet. through film techniques
and the layering of clips, this work
describes a fast-moving network,
loaded with information

182

183

**disclaimer**

every effort has been made to trace copyright holders.
however, if there are any omissions, we will be happy
to rectify them in future editions.

184